MANAGER'S GUIDE TO SHAREPOINT SERVER 2016

TUTORIALS, SOLUTIONS, AND BEST PRACTICES

Heiko Angermann

Apress®

Manager's Guide to SharePoint Server 2016: Tutorials, Solutions, and Best Practices

Heiko Angermann
Nuremberg, Bavaria, Germany

ISBN-13 (pbk): 978-1-4842-3044-2 ISBN-13 (electronic): 978-1-4842-3045-9
https://doi.org/10.1007/978-1-4842-3045-9

Library of Congress Control Number: 2017961852

Cover image by Freepik (`www.freepik.com`)

Managing Director: Welmoed Spahr
Editorial Director: Todd Green
Acquisitions Editor: Susan McDermott
Development Editor: Laura Berendson
Technical Reviewer: Treb Gatte
Coordinating Editor: Rita Fernando
Copy Editor: Michael G. Laraque

Distributed to the book trade worldwide by Springer Science+Business Media New York, 233 Spring Street, 6th Floor, New York, NY 10013. Phone 1-800-SPRINGER, fax (201) 348-4505, e-mail `orders-ny@springer-sbm.com`, or visit `www.springeronline.com`. Apress Media, LLC is a California LLC and the sole member (owner) is Springer Science+Business Media Finance Inc (SSBM Finance Inc). SSBM Finance Inc is a **Delaware** corporation.

For information on translations, please e-mail `rights@apress.com`, or visit `www.apress.com/rights-permissions`.

Apress titles may be purchased in bulk for academic, corporate, or promotional use. eBook versions and licenses are also available for most titles. For more information, reference our Print and eBook Bulk Sales web page at `www.apress.com/bulk-sales`.

Any source code or other supplementary material referenced by the author in this book is available to readers on GitHub via the book's product page, located at `www.apress.com/9781484230442`. For more detailed information, please visit `www.apress.com/source-code`.

Printed on acid-free paper

Apress Business: The Unbiased Source of Business Information

Apress business books provide essential information and practical advice, each written for practitioners by recognized experts. Busy managers and professionals in all areas of the business world—and at all levels of technical sophistication—look to our books for the actionable ideas and tools they need to solve problems, update and enhance their professional skills, make their work lives easier, and capitalize on opportunity.

Whatever the topic on the business spectrum—entrepreneurship, finance, sales, marketing, management, regulation, information technology, among others—Apress has been praised for providing the objective information and unbiased advice you need to excel in your daily work life. Our authors have no axes to grind; they understand they have one job only—to deliver up-to-date, accurate information simply, concisely, and with deep insight that addresses the real needs of our readers.

It is increasingly hard to find information—whether in the news media, on the Internet, and now all too often in books—that is even-handed and has your best interests at heart. We therefore hope that you enjoy this book, which has been carefully crafted to meet our standards of quality and unbiased coverage.

We are always interested in your feedback or ideas for new titles. Perhaps you'd even like to write a book yourself. Whatever the case, reach out to us at editorial@apress.com, and an editor will respond swiftly. Incidentally, at the back of this book, you will find a list of useful related titles. Please visit us at www.apress.com to sign up for newsletters and discounts on future purchases.

—The Apress Business Team

Contents

About the Author

Heiko Angermann is an omni-channel publishing specialist. Recently he is the head of project management at an e-commerce consulting house located in Nuremberg, Germany. Heiko received a B.Eng. in print and media technology (digital publishing) from Stuttgart Media University (HdM), Germany, in 2014 and a Ph.D. in computer engineering from University of the West of Scotland (UWS) in 2017. His research interests are the management and analysis of heterogeneous data in omni-channel context, including metadata management and process management. Before joining UWS, he was a lecturer on content management systems and a researcher at HdM for projects on customer relationship management. Heiko was involved as a SharePoint administrator at a Microsoft gold partner in Stuttgart, Germany, and was involved as a product data manager in terms of enterprise resource planning at two international printing houses located in Bern, Switzerland and Berlin, Germany. Heiko has participated in projects funded by the European Union, German research councils, or enterprises. He has authored or coauthored several publications, including journal articles, conference articles, magazine articles, and workshop articles.

About the Technical Reviewer

Treb Gatte, speaker, author, M.B.A., Business Solutions MVP, MCP, and MCTS, is an internationally recognized project management expert on project management processes, using the Project Server and SharePoint product suites. Treb has 23 years of experience in project management and business process development. In 2013, he was recognized by Microsoft with a Most Valued Professional (MVP) award for contributions to the Project Server community. He has managed large-scale implementations at Wachovia Bank (now Wells Fargo), Microsoft, and Starbucks. Treb has also written three books on Project Server and SharePoint, covering configuration, administration, and day-to-day use.

Treb holds certifications in Project Server and SharePoint configuration. He was formerly a program manager on the Microsoft product team for Project Server. He holds a B.S. in management from Louisiana State University and an M.B.A. from Wake Forest University. His expertise in Power BI and business intelligence enabled Tumble Road to earn a Power BI Showcase partner designation from Microsoft.

Introduction

Over the last few decades, it has become an ever-increasing task to manage the mountains of structured and unstructured data required to run today's businesses. Content management systems (CMS) are the tools of choice to help businesses get their content under control. However, as firms have different claims on CMS, depending on the type of information the firm has to deal with, the type of use, and the type of provision, different available CMS are available that usually focus more or less on different tasks. For example, some CMS focus on managing and publishing content for the web, known as web content management systems (WCMS). Other systems, known as document management systems (DMS), are not concerned with publishing on the web but are specialized for structuring paper-based content within an intranet, and other CMS focus on administrating digital non-paper-based documents, known as digital asset management systems (DAMS). Other CMS, referred to as electronic records management systems (ERMS), manage business records. And, in addition, CMS exist that focus on all the previously mentioned tasks within a single system, known as enterprise content management systems (ECMS). Such systems do not follow a single methodology or idea but have the ability to support enterprises in a holistic manner, namely as a system to depict the strategic and dynamic process inside enterprises.

The CMS Microsoft SharePoint Server (usually abbreviated as SharePoint) focused, with its first releases in 2001 and 2003, on managing documents inside a collaborative environment. However, since the release in 2007, it became a true ECMS, with permanent development and improvements coming with the subsequent releases in 2010, 2013, and 2016. Despite these, however, at the management level, the opportunities as well as limits of SharePoint are often unknown, as a concrete use case of the available features and functionalities

© Heiko Angermann 2017
H. Angermann, *Manager's Guide to SharePoint Server 2016*,
https://doi.org/10.1007/978-1-4842-3045-9_1

is missing. In addition, daily users with or without computer affinity are often overwhelmed by the complexity of this all-around solution, as the palette of functionalities and possibilities is too extensive. For example, the provided site collection templates include overlapping functionalities that make the right choice challenging. The same holds true for the different site collection templates included with applications. In addition, the customizing of SharePoint is often error-prone and time-consuming, as the inheritance of diverse settings is unknown, or the activation of settings that are required to allow customization is missing. In the end, this leads to dissatisfaction and, in the worst case, results in a rejection of the system on two fronts. First, managers who have decided to use SharePoint reject the system, as they do not see its benefits. Second, end users who must employ the system daily are dissatisfied, as the ECMS does not simplify their jobs if the possibilities and limits are unknown, or the system is not in a shape to effectively support daily tasks.

To overcome these challenges, this book provides a hands-on introduction to this leading ECMS. As such, it explains SharePoint—more precisely, its most recent release, Microsoft SharePoint Server 2016—from the perspective of how it can concretely help enterprises in specific, but also general, use cases. In addition, it details, with more focus on management and strategic development, how to impart the possibilities of SharePoint to users, instead of focusing on users with programming skills, as provided in the very comprehensive books introduced by Tony Smith[1] and Olga M. Londer.[2] With the help of understandable tutorials, best practices, and solutions, this book provides transparency regarding what is available but, in turn, the most fitting technologies for a specific business goal, such as managing content for the web, structuring documents, administrating records, and managing assets. Moreover, the different chapters include guidelines for overlapping tasks, such as project management, improving collaboration, managing metadata, access level, etc. With this in mind, the book focuses on four types of practitioners and scholars across domains, as follows:

- **Managers/Consultants,** who decide which CMS will be used to increase the manageability of content in small, medium, and large enterprises. After reading this book, managers and consultants will be able to understand how and where SharePoint can help improve companies' success.

---

[1] Tony Smith, *SharePoint 2016 Users' Guide: Learning Microsoft's Business Collaboration Platform* (New York: Apress, 2017); Penelope Coventry, http://www.apress.com/de/book/9781484222430.

[2] Olga Londer, *Microsoft SharePoint 2016 Step by Step* (Redmond, WA: Microsoft Press, 2016) https://www.microsoftpressstore.com/store/microsoft-sharepoint-2016-step-by-step-9780735697768.

- **Final users**, who use SharePoint for daily business, e.g., users who work together on projects or those who are responsible for editing content. With the help of this book, users of SharePoint will be able to better understand what to do within SharePoint and how to more effectively deal with this ECMS.

- **Site administrators**, who are responsible to customize SharePoint to improve usability and user experience. This type of audience will be able to understand the core elements and applications inside and outside SharePoint used for customizing, and how to improve the sites' functionalities, as well as functionalities of the included applications, libraries, pages, web/template parts, etc.

- **Scholars/Students**, who teach or study the basics of CMS in undergraduate and postgraduate courses with a focus on applied science. Teachers will be able to better explain the use of SharePoint as a collaboration and management platform and, consequently, students will be able to more quickly understand what a CMS provides.

The remainder of the book is organized as follows. In this chapter, an introduction to CMS is given. The scope of CMS is detailed and the differences between the various types of CMS are explained. This includes the differences from a functional perspective (DMS, WCMS, DAMS, ERMS, and ECMS) but also from a license perspective (proprietary vs. open source), as well as from an operative perspective (on-premise vs. cloud computing). The second chapter elaborates ECMS SharePoint by giving details about its basic technology and the features and ideas of the provided templates (site collection, applications). Hands-on tutorials are presented in the third chapter, in which the underlying technology and templates to be used are covered in detail. These tutorials are divided into different use cases having different level of complexity. Through this, use cases for end users, but also use cases for site or site collection administrators are included. Best practice scenarios are presented in the fourth chapter. These include case studies, governance, and tools to improve the usability, manageability, and the look and feel of SharePoint. Solutions for the hands-on tutorials are presented in the fifth chapter. In the sixth chapter, the book finally concludes.

Content Management Systems

Content management is the process of preparing and processing information, whereby a content management system is a software application to support its collaborative management.[3] CMS are used in business to manage documents, simplify web content publishing, enable business transaction traceability, and provide libraries for managing digital assets. First, this chapter presents CMS from a logical perspective. Afterward, the differences between the various functions of different types of CMS are explained.

Logical Components of Content Management Systems

To manage a huge amount of content, each CMS is divided into two logical components: a management processes component on the one side, and a system processes component on the other side (see Figure 1-1).

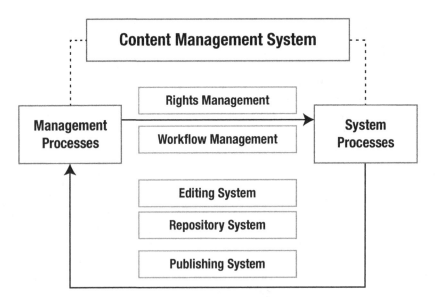

Figure 1-1. Components inside CMS to allow capturing, managing, storing, preserving, and, finally, publishing content

---

[3]Thomas Hess, "Content Management System (CMS)." In Insa Sjurts, ed., *Gabler Lexikon Medienwirtschaft [Gabler Lexicon Media Economics]* (Wiesbaden, Germany: Gabler Verlag, 2011).

The management process component is required to manage the various rights of users and to process workflows from a strategic perspective. It manages the different levels of accessibility and the necessary workflows to manage the information according to the enterprise's needs. It utilizes two sub components:

- **Rights management** is used to structure the different types of users into different groups, called user management. The various user groups are assigned different levels of access, which control authentication and content-based access.

- **Workflow management** is utilized to standardize and automatize the processes inside the system processes but also the processes between the three different system processes.

A system process component is needed to treat the CMS tasks from an operational level, that is, to enable the information management processes. This includes the capturing and management of information, the storage of information to preserve content, and, finally, publication of the information. The process-oriented view is divided into three areas:[4]

- **Editing system** allows content and data to be edited inline. This means that the editing is done inside the CMS, without the use of another application on another machine (personal computer, virtual machine, server, etc.). For example, the editing and formatting of a text or table can be done without using a further text editor or a separate spreadsheet program.

- **Repository system** allows for storage of the captured content. To improve the ability to search information, two different semantic techniques are used: taxonomy and folksonomy. Taxonomy uses hierarchically ordered concepts (also known as terms) to model a domain in a formal way.[5] Such types of metadata have their merits for navigation and for exploring similar items.[6] For storing page-based documents, for example, taxonomy is used to issue the scope of the documents, whereby tags are used to better describe the content of a document. Folksonomy can model a field of interest in an informal way, using

---

[4]"ADDIN ZOTERO_ITEM CSL_CITATION {"citationID")," http://wirtschaftslexikon. gabler.de/Definition/content-management-system-cms.html, accessed March 1, 2017.
[5]David Sánchez and Montserrat Batet, t MRO_ITEM CSL_CITATION {"citationID":"2 pif96fo0u","properties":{"formattedCitation":"{\\rtf*Expert Systems with Applications* 40, 1393ionsms with.
[6]Heiko Angermann and Naeem Ramzan, TaxoPublish: Towards a Solution to Automatically Personalize Taxonomies in E-Catalogs, at *Expert Systems with Applications* 33, 75rt (2016).

keywords (often referred to as tags). This type of semantic structure allows keyword-based search, as it is used to index the search engine.[7] Tags are a quick means of finding specific information. While concepts are generally created by experts, tags can usually be created by any user.

- **Publishing system** makes it possible to publish (deliver) stored information. Again, the type of content distinguishes how publishing is performed. For example, the publishing of information can be done via the Internet, to make it available to anonymous users, inside an intranet, to be available only to known users, or published by another system.

Finding Information

The management of large amount of data has caused a paradigm change in how we access information. The focus of structuring information has changed to finding information based on formal and informal structured data. Finding information involves the following processes:

- **Crawling process** is a regularly performed process ensuring that the queries to be executed can always rely on the relevant data. Therefore, it is necessary to clarify a crawling schedule, which defines the resources and content types that must be crawled, and, of course, how often the crawling is to be performed. Depending on the amount of data, this process is usually performed hourly, daily, or weekly.

- **Indexing process** collects data that has been crawled. Its aim is to organize the crawled data in a structured (indexed) manner. This has the benefit of allowing search queries to be performed in an efficient manner.

- **Querying process** is the last of the search queries performed by the user. This process uses indexed items to ultimately show to the user the items satisfying a query.

- **Raking process** sorts the detected results, depending on the extent to which the single detected items overlap with the performed query. It is also known as relevance. Usually, the more that keywords overlap with the query and the resulted item, the higher the relevance, and the higher it is ranked.

---

[7]Heiko Angermann and Zeeshan Pervez and Naeem Ramzan, TaxoSemantics: Assessing similarity between multi-word expressions for extending e-catalogs, at Decision Support Systems 98, (2017). http://www.sciencedirect.com/science/article/pii/S016792361730060X.

Search Experience

Today, a good search experience is crucial for information management, in addition to providing intuitive navigation. This is because the amount of data is increasing rapidly, but the huge amount of information stored on the internet is mainly distributed over only a few platforms, such as Google, Facebook, YouTube, and Yahoo, which increased rapidly in importance over the last years.[8] Because of this, different approaches have been developed for optimizing search, i.e., on-page and off-page optimization.

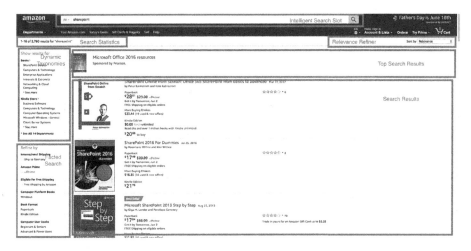

Figure 1-2. Techniques for finding products on Amazon

To allow a good search experience, the underlying search engines must consider different types of search result representation (e.g., images, products), handle different types of data (e.g., text, figures, metadata), interpret the search query, recognize how results should be ordered, and should allow additional techniques for filtering in detail. The leading retailing firms provide search-driven applications that satisfy the previously mentioned criteria. This means that the focus is strongly on finding products by using the search slot. In turn, the search slot must interact in an intelligent manner, and other metadata-driven search techniques must be supported, depending on the query performed inside the slot. The leading retailing firm Amazon, for example, is providing all state-of-the-art techniques for helping customers to find the desired products with a search-driven application, summarized in Figure 1-2:

---

[8]The Internet Map, http://internet-map.net/, accessed June 1, 2017.

- **Intelligent Search (Slot)** can suggest products. If a customer begins to write a phrase, the search engine can automatically suggest products by automatically completing that phrase. In addition, the intelligent search slot can tolerate phrases that include spelling errors, compare synonyms, and handle phrases typed in upper or lower case.

- **Search Statistics** show the customer how many relevant products are found, based on the performed search query.

- **Relevance Refiner** lets the customer sort the resulted products in different ways. For example, the results can be sorted by: best results, popularity, price, or novelty.

- **Top Search Results** and **Search Results** finally show the products found. The previously mentioned results are included at the top of the list, whereas other results are presented below. Usually, a fee must be paid to be a top result.

- **Dynamic Taxonomies** and **Faceted Search** provide a customer the opportunity to strictly refine search results. Therefore, products that are part of a specific subcategory can be filtered (by dynamic taxonomy), or products satisfying a specific metadata tag can be filtered (by faceted search).

Besides the above-mentioned techniques, the ability to handle language is the most crucial element of search engines. The reason is that typing phrases into the search slot can cause many problems. The biggest problem is that some phrases have the same meaning, known as synonyms. For example, the words *watch* and *clock* can be considered synonyms. Because of this, the search engine must be able to recognize if a phrase is a synonym of another phrase and show both results. In contrast, phrases exist that have an opposite meaning. These are known as homonyms. For example, the word *ice* has multiple meanings. The search engine must also have the right level of tolerance, meaning that it must accommodate both the users employing specialist terms to filter for products, as well as others using very general phrases. Also, users employing negating terms must also be considered. In addition, the search engine must be able to apply root words and handle abbreviations.

Navigation

Navigation on a web site includes control elements and links to help users navigate through the information management system (content management system, e-commerce system, enterprise resource planning, etc.) and, ultimately, to simplify the user's orientation.

Metadata Techniques

Traditionally, using folders (e.g., inside file directories) has supported the structuring of information inside information management systems, such as documents inside DMS. Therefore, the folders are used to simulate a hierarchical order of the data. These orders are classified by a name that is defined by a nomenclature or, informally, without any rules. In addition, some information (metadata) is assigned to these folders, such as the date of creation, the date of the last modification, or the size of the included documents. The technique of using folders provides a clear structure, as well as a good control over the documents. However, storage is too inflexible for most use cases. It is not intuitive, and, of course, users have to perform many clicks to reach the desired information. A much quicker way of finding the desired information is provided by using filters. As the information management systems provide lists to collect data, e.g., documents, filters can be created, depending on specific information, for different users, for sorting, etc. This allows more intuitive structuring of data, based on the information included and, ultimately, reduces the time to find the desired information. However, for effective filtering, data must have the correct information (e.g., realized with using a nomenclature). Creating the wrong filters is misleading, and filters must be used correctly. To automatically provide predefined filters, another technique, called views, is used inside information management systems. Such views can rely on existing filters and provide for single use cases, or single users, exactly the information required. However, with this, other drawbacks exist. First, only predefined views can be used, and unless a user is an administrator, further filtering is usually not supported, and becomes complicated. Often, many useless views may have been created, and data has to be stored correctly to use the views effectively.

As information management platforms are now more diverse and fragmented than ever before, presenting users an overload of information across different platforms and channels (social media, e-commerce, forums, content management, etc.), the aforementioned techniques are no longer sufficient. To overcome this information overload, to support an intuitive structuring of the information, and to finally help people find the desired information, two metadata techniques are provided in current information management systems: taxonomy and folksonomy. On the one hand, the lightweight method, folksonomy, is applied in the form of informal keywords to data, products, blogs, conversations, reviews, etc. This technique has enjoyed high acceptance by users, as they can define their own tags, the handling is intuitive, and the realization is quick. However, as there are no restrictions for creating tags, the folksonomies contain semantic ambiguities and synonyms. On the other hand, the formal method, taxonomy, uses hierarchically ordered concepts. Taxonomy can be created by going from the most general to the most specific concepts, or vice versa. In addition, the concepts of the taxonomy can be classified according to the process being considered, the organizational structure, or by using a standard taxonomy. Such a metadata-driven technique has evident advantages to facilitate users' navigation through large data corpuses. As the concepts are formally controlled, the structure is consistent, and the concepts are semantically rich. However, as the taxonomy is usually created by experts who know the domain of interest in detail, this technique is often lacking in user acceptance. The reason is that for some users, it is not intuitive, as every user has other ways to structure a domain, but each user is offered the identical, inflexible taxonomy.

As both metadata techniques have their own benefits and drawbacks, both are combined in practice. On the one hand, taxonomy ensures that each document is assigned the formally correct concept. Because of this, it is important that the taxonomy be not too fine-grained, to have a clear differentiation between concepts. On the other hand, folksonomy ensures that finding the desired information is intuitive. So, in the end, each item (document, data, etc.) should be assigned with a formal concept defining the general area of the item and informal tags giving more detailed information about the item.

Workflows

With the help of workflows, enterprises can ensure consistent business processes. In addition, as workflows perform fully or semiautomatically, enterprises can automatize and standardize specific tasks for improving operational effectiveness and productivity. For users, workflows allow focusing on the actual required tasks. In practice, workflows are used inside CMS for editing documents, managing tasks, or creating and approving pages to be published on the web.

From a technical perspective, workflows can be considered a stringing together of single tasks or events, whereby each task results in a single result. Two types of workflows can be distinguished. For realizing linear procedures having no loops, sequential workflows exist. Each task is followed by another, wherein the former task cannot be repeated. For realizing more complex workflows, so-called state-machine workflows exist. By this, loops between tasks can be considered, as well as relationships between tasks. No matter which type of workflow is used, each workflow consists of the following three main phases:

- **Association** is the first phase to be performed. This assigns a workflow to a specific object, e.g., an item inside a list, a document inside a library, a page to be approved, etc.

- **Initiation** is the second phase. Here, the workflow is started. This can be performed manually or in an automatic manner, e.g., if a new item is created or an item is modified.

- **Execution** is the third and final phase. This means that the different tasks/steps of the workflow are performed, e.g., sending an e-mail, collecting feedback, giving a new status to an item, etc.

Types of Content Management Systems

During the last decades, different types of CMS have been manufactured according to the technical progress achieved and, associated with it, the different requirements of varying business cases and sectors. All technically different CMS use the same previously mentioned system and management processes but vary in their ability to capture information, store content, manage the processes, preserve information, and publish content on different channels and devices. The following four types of CMS are distinct: document management systems (DMS), web content management systems (WCMS), digital asset management systems (DAM), and electronic records management systems (ERMS). Combining the single types lead to a fifth type: the enterprise content management system (ECMS).

Document Management Systems

DMS help firms to capture, store, and manage (track) paper-based content and preserve documents.[9] For example, documents stored in the closed Portable Document Format (PDF), slides stored as editable PowerPoint files, or editable text documents stored as Word files can be effectively managed inside a DMS, including sharing, approval, editing, etc.

The main purpose of a DMS is to support the collaborative creation of documents and their structured storage. Within workflow management, the business processes to create, store, preserve, and share documents are considered. For example, the preparation/writing of the document, e.g., a user manual, is considered the first step. The document's approval or rejection by

---

[9]Association for Information and Image Management (AIIM), "ADDIN ZOTERO_ITEM CSL_CITATION {"c"A www.aiim.org/What-Is-Document-Imaging#, 2017.

a coeditor can be considered a second step. If the document is approved, the proofreading is performed as a third step, before the document is approved by the sponsoring editor, published, and, ultimately, preserved. Within rights management, the type of contribution to the document is considered. In our example, the author and proofreader are eligible to write and edit the user manual but cannot approve/reject it and, of course, cannot share it with the printing company. Conversely, the coeditor can approve/reject the document, leave comments to the author if the document is rejected, and send the document to the printing company, if it is approved, but she/he cannot write the document or make changes. To allow such scenarios, the DMS must include the following techniques[10]:

- **Check-in/check-out** allows simultaneous editing, as well as coauthoring.[11] Check in of a document means that the file is uploaded into the DMS. The document is asserted with metadata, such as the date of creation, date of last edit, author, number of pages, etc. To check out a document means that the file still exists inside the DMS but cannot be edited. The reason is that another person has recently edited it. However, after editing, this person will again check in the document. For example, after the author corrects the document according to the feedback of the proofreader, the document will be checked out.

- **Versioning and annotating** enables control of the differences between single versions of the document and the document life cycle. After every change to the document, a new version is created. The versioning process usually distinguishes between two types of versions. Major versions indicate comprehensive changes to the document; minor versions indicate small changes to the document. For example, to distinguish between draft versions, minor versions are created. Conversely, to differentiate between approved versions, major versions are created. To always be able to come back to the prior version, the DMS also utilizes what is known as the roll-back feature. Annotating allows for leaving comments to each version of the document, e.g., to communicate required changes.

---

[10]Ibid.
[11]Microsoft, "ADDIN ZOTERO_ITEM CSL_CITATION {"citation https://support.office.com/en-us/article/Document-collaboration-and-co-authoring-ee1509b4-1f6e-401e-b04a-782d26f564a4, 2017.

- **Audit trail** enables users to control which person has contributed what to the document, for example, to determine why a document was processed incorrectly or who has accessed the file.

- **Automatic tagging** means that the document is automatically assigned with related metadata—the tags. Through this, the user does not have to create the tags manually, as they are automatically retrieved, based on the content of the document.

Web Content Management Systems

WCMS help firms, organizations, and private persons to capture, manage, store, preserve, and publish content as web pages on the Internet.[12]

The main benefit of using WCMS is the collaborative creation of web pages, which allows for dynamic (queried) content on pages, user management, and, for most of these systems, almost no programming skills are required to publish a web site. As with managing documents, the workflows performing inside WCMS focus on the processes to create, approve, and publish web sites. However, for managing web content, the processes to remove web pages, to archive content and pages, and to create/remove dynamic content on web pages have to be considered. For example, suppose that a marketing assistant is writing about her firm's new product. This copy has to appear alongside the new product as well as on the start page. However, if another product is more recent, copy about the previous product must disappear. Within rights management, WCMS generally distinguishes between only a few internal users on the one hand, e.g., staff that creates and fills the web sites, and a huge number of external users on the other hand, e.g., clients, peers, and prospective clients who only read the information and are not logged in to the site. In summary, compared to an intranet platform, the main differences are that anonymous access must be supported, as well as multilingualism, the focus is on layout and design, and information must be approved before finally being published on the web. However, if the WCMS allow the creation of a forum or blog, external users are also allowed to contribute to the web pages, e.g., in the form of reviews or blog entries. The key features of WCMS are as follows[13]:

---

[12]AIIM, "ADDIN ZOTERO_ITEM CSL_CITAT www.aiim.org/What-is-Web-20#, 2017.
[13]Ibid.

- **Design of web sites** is usually performed with templates. Templates control the position and the look and feel of different blocks that appear as a complete site. For example, a product-page template can include a block as a header, to display the name of the product; an image block on the left side below the headline, to illustrate the product; and a text block on the right side below the headline, to describe the product in detail.

- **Organization of web sites** requires different types of techniques. First, whether the recent site subsumes another site must be defined, and, with this, the navigation below its parent site. Second, metadata is required to administrate the site, with the help of formal terms and informal tags. Such metadata defines when the site was created, by whom it was created, when it will be removed, which version is published, etc.

- **Web site creation workflows** allow for standardizing, controlling, and automating the complete web site life cycle, including its creation, and the archiving of single web sites, in addition to the removal of outdated content. An example is a site that has been created by a marketing member, approved by the head of marketing and then automatically published after its approval.

- **Dynamic content inside web pages** enables the use of already existing information inside blocks on other sites. In our example, the headline and image of the product page site will most likely also occur on the site summarizing all available products, whereby its description only occurs on the product page site itself. However, if the product is new, the image and the description of the product may also occur on the main/home page of the company.

Digital Asset Management System

DAMS, often referred to also as media asset management, supports enterprises in tasks concerning the organization, storage, sharing, and retrieval of assets. Such digital files can be any type of media, such as photos, video, audio, and slides.[14] However, page-based documents are often considered as assets as well, because they require the same processes of document management.

---

[14]Webdam, "ADDIN ZOTERO_ITEM CSL_CITATION {"ci https://webdam.com/what-is-digital-asset-management/, December 12, 2016.

Through using DAMS, firms are provided with a centralized digital library from which to create, manage, store, and track assets in a structured way inside a collaborative environment. The workflow management must consider the different stakeholders who create the assets, approve the assets, and utilize the assets for publishing and sharing. Using photos as an example, the process of taking a photo is the first step. The image processing in the pre-press department is the second step. The approval by a senior editor is the third step. And the submission of the photo to a printing company is the fourth step. Within rights management, DAMS perform like a system for managing paper-based documents. The key features of DAMS are the following:

- **Automatic converting** means that during the import and export of assets, these are automatically converted into another file format. This is important, as when publishing the asset on different channels, different resolutions are required. In addition, the publishing is performed using closed formats, whereby the editing is performed using open file formats. For example, a file in a Portable Network Graphics (PNG) format is exported as a Joint Photographic Experts Group (JPEG) file to be used on a digital device but is exported as a high-resolution Portable Document Format (PDF) file and is edited using Adobe Photoshop file format.

- **Automatic indexing** and **categorization of media** is necessary to help users find the assets they need.[15] Again, metadata in the form of semantic technologies (taxonomy and folksonomy) is crucial.

- **Processing and review process** is performed using workflows. Similar to managing documents and web sites, the workflows usually treat the complete life cycle of assets.

- **Visualization and rendering** are crucial today in multichannel applications, meaning the use of different devices and channels to display and finally publish an asset.

Electronic Records Management Systems

ERMS help enterprises to control the distribution, use, maintenance, and disposition of records to document business transactions and activities.[16]

---

[15]Elizabeth Ferguson Keathley, *Digital Asset Management—Content Architectures, Project Management, and Creating Order Out of Media Chaos*, (New York, Apress, 2014).
[16]AIIM, "ADDIN ZOTERO_ITEM CSL_CITATION {"citationID""A www.aiim.org/What-is-ERM-Electronic-Records-Management#, 2017.

The main advantage to using an ERMS is that enterprises can document their business processes and transactions. The key features of ERMS are as follows:[17]

- **Unique identifiers** ensure that each record in a database is assigned with a primary key existing only once over a set of objects. In addition, such identifiers are used to set objects in relation to other objects. An example is that a service provider receives a unique identifier, as does a customer. The e-mails (records) coming from the service provider also receive unique identifiers. This means that the other two identifiers mentioned are used as so-called foreign keys, through which the complete conversation and its participants can be clearly identified.

- **Digital signature** means that a record is assigned with a secret and public key generated with the help of an asymmetric cryptosystem. This ensures that the integrity and authorship of a record cannot be violated. E.g., the contract between the provider and the customer is assigned with a key that reveals the creator of the document.

- **Audit trails** handle the examination of processes, activities, and results regarding the fulfillment of predefined requirements, norms, and standards.[18] The audit trail itself is the method used to control and document the attempted and actual acts of users during a specific time period.

- **Refresh and migrate** are necessary, as records contain a firm's sensitive information and, in some branches, must be stored for extended periods, even decades. This feature ensures long-term accessibility to the records, as it periodically refreshes and migrates the database supporting the ERMS.

Enterprise Content Management Systems

The aggregation of the four types of CMS within one environment is known as enterprise content management systems (ECMS). As each of the above-mentioned types is already a complex process, managing enterprise content requires an ongoing and evolving strategy to achieve business goals. This is

---

[17]Ibid.
[18]Helmut Siller, "Audit Trail," Springer Gabler, http://wirtschaftslexikon.gabler.de/Definition/audit-trail.html, accessed March 1, 2017.

realized through a combination of methods, strategies, and technologies to capture, manage, store, preserve, and publish information (see Table 1-1). ECMS support enterprises in systematically collecting and organizing any type of information to be used by a designated audience in a collaborative environment, e.g., clients, departments, agile project teams, etc., as summarized in Figure 1-3.[19]

Table 1-1. Enterprise content management life cycles[20]

Life Cycle Stage	Disciplines and Software Subsystems
Capture	Capture
Manage	Document Management, Web Content Management, Digital Asset Management, Workflows, Collaboration, E-mail Management, Business Process Management
Store	File Systems, Repositories, Databases, Data Warehouses
Preserve	Electronic Records Management
Deliver	Organization and Access to Information, Enterprise Search, Distribution

---

[19]AIIM, "ADDIN ZOTERO_ITEM CSL_CITATION {"citationID""A www.aiim.org/What-is-ECM-Enterprise-Content-Management#, 2017.
[20]VerDDIN ZOTERO_ITEM CSL_CITATION {"citationID":"2gmf2r29lc","properties":{ "formattedCitatient (Part 2)," Athento, http://smartdocumentmanagement.athento.com/2013/12/enterprise-content-management-and-the-management-of-content-life-cycle-part-two.html, 2013, accessed March 3, 2017.

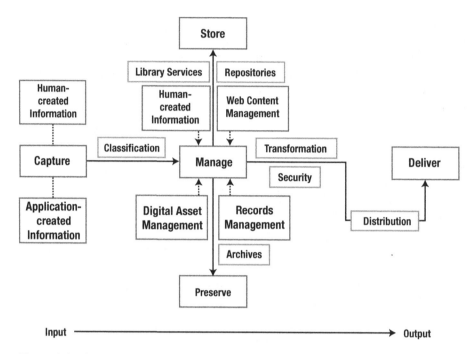

Figure 1-3. Enterprise content management roadmap, courtesy of AIIM[21]

The main benefit of using ECMS is that the enterprise establishes a cumulative system, rather than single systems, to capture, store, manage, preserve, and deliver different types of content. With an ECMS, storage costs are reduced, as redundant content is eliminated; operating costs are decreased, through workflows performing without system interruption; and productivity and efficiency are enhanced, as users get exactly what they need at the right time.[22] To achieve this, ECMS must include the following features[23]:

- **Collaboration** has to be supported, to accommodate a potentially huge number of users and to prevent loss of information. The more information from inside and outside the system that can be captured inside ECMS, the

[21]AIIM, op cit.

[22]John F. Mancini, M CSL_CITATION {"citationID":ecvAIIM, http://info.aiim.org/digital-landfill/newaiimo/2010/02/25/todays-opinion-leader-is-chris-walker-an-independent-information-management-consultant-his-expertise-includes-business-and, February 25, 2010, accessed March 1, 2017.

[23]Mary Ann Lorkowski, OEnterprise Content Management (ECM)—The Key Features You Need to Know SlideShare, www.slideshare.net/mdlorkowski/ecm-key-features-you-need-to-know, January 15, 2012.

better. This includes documents, tasks, calendars, blogs, wikis, e-mail integration, and the capability to manage projects, teams, departments, etc.

- **Portal** means that users are not restricted only to a user account to log in/log out of tasks they are performing. In ECMS, users receive their own profile, to maintain information about themselves, such as education, work experience, contributed projects, interest, etc. In addition, they can connect to other users, create their own sites, and have their own repository to share content.

- **Search** within ECMS must ensure that a huge amount of information, which is heterogeneous according to type and format, can be found. To improve searchability, search engines must be capable of allowing keyword-based search, must be scalable, and faceted search must be enabled.

- **Content management** includes managing documents, managing records, administrating assets, and managing content to be published on the web.

- **Business forms and processes** must enable users to capture information in browsers and allow nonsequential workflows to handle more complex processes over different subtasks. In addition, back-end integration must be enabled, as well as single sign-on.

- **Business intelligence** is required to analyze information. This includes the integration of sensitive data, server-based spreadsheets, data visualization, and key performance indicators.

Types of License and Provision Models

In addition to the technical aspects of the different types of CMS, the systems can also vary according to license type and the type operating the CMS, especially since the advent of cloud computing. This section presents the types of licensing that exist and those that can be used to operate a CMS.

Proprietary vs. Open Source Systems

Regarding the different license models, CMS can be distinguished by two main categories: proprietary CMS and open source CMS.[24] However, one system may be available not only as a single license type. Usually, applications are available in various license types, which differ as to the type of service model and the range of implemented features.

Proprietary CMS require a fee, as the manufacturer of the CMS owns the rights to the application, and the user buys permission to use the CMS.[25] The advantages of using a fee-based CMS are that support is ensured, the system is stable and built for enterprise needs, and the manufacturer makes sure that training for users and administrators is given. The drawbacks of utilizing a proprietary CMS are that you have to pay a fee to use the system, the number of available developers and administrators is lower, most modules are also fee-based, and the number of communities and forums is lower, as not everyone can use it.

Open source CMS, in contrast, are not fee-based.[26] Such systems can be used, customized, and further developed by anyone and for any purpose. The advantages of using an open source CMS are that the system is free and a large community of developers, administrators, and users is available. However, support is not assured when using an open source CMS, and the systems are often not stable, as bugs are sometimes included. Pure open source CMS are often not suitable for enterprise needs. Because of this, manufacturers of open source CMS usually provide additionally what is known as an enterprise version, or suite, which is fee-based. Using this, an open source CMS can be reserved for private persons or smaller firms, and the aforementioned enterprise version CMS retained for medium and large businesses.

On-Premise vs. Cloud Computing

With regard to the different types of systems operating and provisioning the CMS, two main categories, each with its own benefits and drawbacks, can be distinguished: on-premise and cloud computing (usually abbreviated as cloud). Again, one application may not only be available solely as one provision type, but as different models, which vary in the degree to which they use their own or foreign hardware.

---

[24]Lahle Wolfe, _ITEM CSL_CITATION {"citationID":"24I557qulo","prop The Balance, www.thebalance.com/an-overview-of-types-of-content-management-systems-3515920, July 17, 2017.

[25]Stephen Zucknovich, A Classic Debate: Open Source vs. Proprietary CMS for Fund Management Websites Kurtosys, https://blog.kurtosys.com/a-classic-debate-open-source-vs-proprietary-cmss-for-asset-management-websites/, April 9, 2015.

[26]Ibid.

On-premise CMS, whether open source or proprietary, are performed on hardware administrated by the user and not provided by the manufacturer of the CMS. The user (e.g., an enterprise) has to provide its own server farm that is static according to the used hardware. It can rent the server farm from another service provider but still must provide its own resources to manage it. Logically, on-premise systems normally adhere to what is called a user license, or, if the system is not open source, a per-server license that is billed annually. This type of provision has been the dominant model since the advent of cloud computing but has lost its attraction in the last decade. The reason is that it provides high control, high adaptability, and high data sensitivity, and ensures that data stays in-house, but the investment costs are high, as are the costs for administration, and the farm is less scalable.[27]

Cloud computing means that CMS do not perform processes on their own hardware but, rather, on hardware provided by another source, for example, the system provider. As a result, investment costs are decreased; hardware is highly scalable in its resources and, therefore, flexible regarding costs for hardware; users require less effort to administrate the CMS farm; and costs are very transparent. Licensing is usually billed per user and is paid monthly or annually. However, when using CMS "in the cloud," you create dependencies of the provider; the legal situation is often unclear, as different countries have different laws; data sensitivity decreases; and, of course, the user has less control over the CMS and the included data.[28] In cloud computing, three different models are differentiated, depending on what is outsourced: platform-as-a-service (PaaS), software-as-a-service (SaaS), and infrastructure-as-a-service (IaaS).

Evaluation and Research Methodologies

For finding the specific CMS that best fits the enterprise's needs, a structured selection process has to be performed. This process is usually performed in five steps, which the enterprise can perform itself or be supported by a consultancy firm or by established market research reports:

1. The market of existing systems has to be scanned, and a criteria catalog has to be established. This catalog should include general criteria, such as highlighting the targets that are pursued with the system to be

---

[27]Louis Columbus and Greg Doud, "Cloud vs. On-Premise: Making the Best Decision for Your Complex Selling System," SlideShare, https://www.slideshare.net/LouisColumbus/cloud-vs-onpremise-making-the-best-decision-for-your-complex-selling-system, October 12, 2012.
[28]Ibid.

implemented, establishing the existing processes, defining how the system will be used, and, of course, clarifying the budget frame. This frame will mainly be influenced by the costs for licenses (if not open source), the costs for migrating and implementing the system, those for additional hardware, support, and training the users. In addition, functional criteria should be addressed, including scenarios to evaluate and test the functionalities of the systems regarding the established criteria.

2. A call for tender should be performed. This means providing potential service providers with the criteria catalog created in the previous step. The provision should be performed by using structured questionnaires, instead of having an unorganized conversation. Alternatively, this can be discussed with potential service providers; manufactures can be consulted directly; market studies can be used; or consultants can support this step. In turn, providers, manufacturers, or consultants will be responsible for answering questions regarding the catalog and, ultimately, for performing a conditional examination.

3. Based on the call for tender, the enterprises usually make a preselection. Afterward, a second discussion with the service providers is performed. Here, the service providers present how the required criteria can be addressed using their system. This presentation usually includes only very high-performing or very attractive features, which is why it is often referred to as a "beauty contest."

4. After another selection based on the preceding step, a further step is required, detailing how the criteria will actually be addressed. This is usually performed by installing the system and by developing prototypes. Therefore, a demonstration is required, and providers create a proof of concept as to how they will meet the requirements regarding time and budget.

5. Based on the criteria catalog and the performed selections, only a few providers should remain, usually a maximum of three. For all providers, a ranking list is compiled, and the prices for setting up the system are discussed in detail. Finally, a specification sheet is created, documenting which features are part of the project.

Criteria Catalog

CMS criteria catalogs, or software catalogs in general, can be created by breaking down the different aspects of the information management system into requirements and summarizing those into categories. In the end, such catalogs include requirements that must be fulfilled to satisfy the enterprise's needs. In addition, each criterion is usually weighted according to its importance. For example, the firm can establish such user-specific criterion as capacity, workflows, and group specificity, wherein group specificity is most important (ranked ten out of ten in importance), but capacity is less important (seven out of ten in importance). The most-widely used criteria and subcriteria used for evaluating CMS are the following:

- **General criteria** include criteria about overall conditions. The manufacturer is included as subcriterion, as it is important that it function over a long period in a stable manner. The license model is considered a subcriterion, as some systems can be open source. The documentation of the system is also important, as users will rely on this. The expandability of the system is also considered a sub criterion, as some systems provide modules to expand the system, whereas others require additional techniques to be developed from scratch.

- **Architecture and infrastructure** consider the very technical criteria. These include subcriteria to review the server landscape—for example, if it is more or less complex and stable. In addition, often included in these criteria are how data and information can be archived, how backups can be performed, and how good data security can be ensured.

- **Content creation** considers mostly the functional criteria. This includes the subcriteria of how content can be created, if different types of templates and layouts are provided, if the front-end design of the system can be customized quickly, if different types of data are allowed, and, of course, if the system is able to provide a good search experience, as well as intuitive link and metadata management/integration.

- **User management** is another criterion that is often part of CMS criteria catalogs. This is important, as, usually, large numbers of users employ the system. Therefore, it is important to consider the user capacity, the ability to manage different permission levels and roles, and to ensure an authentication process that lets people see only what is allowed.

- **Workflows** are required to automatize and standardize the different tasks to be performed within the system. Through this, it is important that different types of workflows are provided out of the box, if the workflows can be customized, and whether they can really cover complex tasks automatically.

Market Research Reports

Market research reports also consider the requirements that a system must fulfill and compare the fulfillment of different CMS. The two most important and well-known fee-based market research reports are provided by Gartner Inc. (www.gartner.com) and Forrester Research, Inc. (www.forrester.com). Each of the two companies uses a proprietary research methodology to identify the best performing systems.

- **Gartner** provides the Gartner magic quadrant research methodology. It classifies the different systems according to their ability to execute the different requirements and their completeness of vision. This results in four types of systems, listed according to their ability to fulfill requirements: leaders (high ability, high completeness), visionaries (high completeness, low ability), challengers (high ability, low completeness), and niche players (low ability, low completeness).[29] Through this, the quadrant can clearly identify the position of competing players in a specific technology market. Regarding the right choice of CMS, the following quadrants are most important: social software, portals, enterprise search, enterprise content management, business process analysis, business intelligence, content collaboration, and web content management.

- **Forrester** provides the Forrester wave research methodology. In each wave, the criteria to grade a system's offerings, as well as a score for each criterion, are provided. To do this, it relies on the participation of four types of contributors: the analyst, who determines

---

[29]Gartner Inc. "Methodology Guide: Gartner Magic Quadrant", ar www.gartner.com/technology/research/methodologies/research_mq.jsp, accessed March 1, 2017.

the criteria; the research associate, who manages the research process and communicates with vendors; a vendor's response team, which comprises the contacts to vendors; and customers who share experiences with the CMS.[30] Each wave classifies the different CMS according to its current offering and its completeness of strategy. At the end, users are presented four types of CMS, listed according their fulfillment of criteria and how this is weighted, as follows: leaders (strong strategy, and strong offering), strong performers (strong to medium strategy, and strong to medium offering), contenders (medium to low strategy, and medium to low offering), and risky bets (low to strong strategy, and low to strong offering). In addition, the wave also reflects the market presence. It does this by differentiating between full vendor participation and incomplete vendor participation.

Crowd-sourced (non-fee-based) research reports exist but are less extensive and less controlled, as anyone, regardless of knowledge and experience, can contribute to these reports. The two most comprehensive crowd-sourced reports are provided by G2 Crowd (www.g2crowd.com), which uses a similar methodology as Gartner, and Trust Radius (www.trustradius.com), which uses what are known as trust maps.

Conclusion

This chapter has provided informative introduction to the general principles of content management. It has included an overview of the different types of existing systems (DMS, WCMS, DAM, ERMS, ECMS), as well as the different components used within such systems. In addition, this chapter has reviewed recent types of license and provision models, including proprietary systems, open source systems, on-premise systems, and cloud computing. This chapter has also presented different methodologies to evaluate the market and specific systems. A novel criteria catalog has been presented, prior to pointing out various market research reports.

---

[30]Forrester "The Forrester Wave Methodology Guide, Gu www.forrester.com/marketing/policies/forrester-wave-methodology.html, 2013.

SharePoint Technology

Microsoft SharePoint Server, often referred to simply as SharePoint, is the enterprise content management system (ECMS) developed and distributed by the Microsoft Corporation (www.microsoft.com). SharePoint combines capabilities to manage content intended to be published on web sites, features to effectively manage paper-based documents, technologies to administrate electronic records, and functionalities to manage digital assets, all inside one uniform system. The latest release of SharePoint was in 2016, named Microsoft SharePoint Server 2016 or, in short, SharePoint 2016.[1] From the introduction of SharePoint in 2001, SharePoint 2016 represents the fifth successive release of the product. With each release, Microsoft has substantially improved the platform, by picking up the most influential trends in information technology and constantly implementing those trends within SharePoint. Therefore, SharePoint focuses not only on functional trends, such as integrating social media features, but also on technical trends, such as providing SharePoint as a cloud computing service instead of one available only on-premise, or improving the graphical user interface (GUI) by providing more branding features.

---

[1]Seth Patton, "SharePoint 2016 RTM and the Future of SharePoint Event," Microsoft Office Blogs, https://blogs.office.com/2016/03/14/sharepoint-2016-rtm-and-the-future-of-sharepoint-event/, March 14, 2016.

© Heiko Angermann 2017
H. Angermann, *Manager's Guide to SharePoint Server 2016*,
https://doi.org/10.1007/978-1-4842-3045-9_2

The first release of Microsoft SharePoint in 2001 was named Microsoft SharePoint Portal Server, or, in short, SharePoint 2001.[2] SharePoint 2001 provided a pure platform to manage paper-based documents, i.e., a document management system (DMS), which was supported through minimal collaboration features. The strategy was to provide a portal solution to enterprises, instead of having isolated applications on personal computers and ultimately storing the documents inside file directories, which do not support automatic versioning and annotating, check-in/check-out, automatic tagging, and audit trail. The next release, named Microsoft Office SharePoint Portal Server 2003, had the same focus, but the range of features was supplemented by the My Site technology. The My Site technology was strongly inspired by the emergence of Web 2.0 and social media platforms like Myspace. With this, the My Site feature greatly improved the collaboration capabilities of SharePoint 2003, by providing techniques to improve social interaction between users, for example, by giving each user the opportunity to create his/her own social profile, and by giving them the possibility to follow other users, etc. The biggest improvement in SharePoint was achieved with the release in 2007 of Microsoft Office SharePoint Server 2007. This was during the era when SharePoint became a comprehensive IT platform and, finally, a complete ECMS. In contrast to the releases in 2001 and 2003, comprehensive techniques are now integrated to create individual web sites, as provided by WCMS. In addition, techniques are integrated to focus also on the management of non-paper-based documents, and techniques to effectively administrate business records have been provided. In addition, and based on the afore mentioned improvements, an updated search center was included, as were business processes and forms and techniques to support business intelligence (BI). In the following release, introduced in 2010, SharePoint supported multi-browsing (platform and device-independent browsing), My Site was improved, and a new user interface provided better usability. The new improvements were based on the emergence of cross-media and the success of new social media platforms like Facebook and Twitter. This version was named Microsoft SharePoint Server 2010. The release introduced in 2013, named Microsoft SharePoint Server 2013, again featured improvements to increase usability. From a user perspective, the main improvements were to the user interface, the support of drag and drop, and the ability to now follow and share documents, sites, persons, etc. With the most recent release, Microsoft SharePoint Server 2016, the focus is on the architecture of SharePoint and the underlying provision model. Now, SharePoint is not only available on-premise but also in the cloud. This version is available as a standalone enterprise content management system and also as an Office 365 application.

---

[2]John P., "Introducing the SharePoint 2016 Readiness Guide: What's New in SharePoint 2016?" AvePoint Blog, www.avepoint.com/blog/avepoint-blog/introducing-sharepoint-2016-readiness-guide-whats-new-sharepoint-2016/, January 13, 2016.

The aim of this chapter is to discuss the underlying technologies of the most recent release of SharePoint theoretically, but also to consider the possibilities and limitations of SharePoint 2016. The first section of this chapter begins by detailing the technology of SharePoint. This includes a discussion of the applications provided, the user interface, and the My Site technology. In the subsequent section, the available templates in SharePoint will be covered. This includes a discussion of which types of templates exist, how these are different, and for which scenario is which template most suitable.

SharePoint Technology

Since the third release of SharePoint in 2007, it has been an ECMS. With each release of SharePoint, new techniques have been implemented, and the existing functionalities constantly improved. To do this, Microsoft considers the trends in the IT sector and transfers those into its ECMS. Because of the constant improvement, SharePoint is one of the most comprehensive ECMS, according to the related market research reports published by the research institutions Gartner Inc. and Forrester Research Inc. This section presents the underlying technologies of SharePoint. It includes a discussion of the basic elements of SharePoint, one about the technology of SharePoint, an explanation of My Site, and, finally, an explanation of the different administration levels.

Basic Elements

In contrast to other ECMS, SharePoint does not illustrate its ECMS capabilities as recommended by the Association for Image and Information Management (AIIM) but inside an autarchy model, called the SharePoint Wheel. With the improvements of the last five releases, the wheel has correspondingly changed, as illustrated in Table 2-1. The recent release, Microsoft SharePoint Server 2016, combines six core capabilities inside the wheel:[3]

- **Sites** provides templates to manage the different types of content, as well as the users themselves. Different templates exist to improve collaboration, enterprise tasks, and publishing. In addition, high granular rights management is provided, and an individual site for each user (My Site).

---

[3]Himanshu Sharma, "Three Types of SharePoint Customers, Which Type Are You?," Trigent Blog, https://blog.trigent.com/three-types-of-sharepoint-customers-which-type-are-you/, June 1, 2014, accessed March 19, 2017.

- **Composites** aims to improve the efficiency of users and teams. This is done through techniques providing forms to create and edit content directly in the browser. In addition, it allows for metadata techniques and the integration of workflows to automatize tasks and reduce error rates.

- **Insights** are capabilities to analyze data. Here, the focus is on business intelligence services. This includes the integration of server-based Excel spreadsheets into SharePoint, to visualize data using dashboards, and the ability to initiate performance measurements, so-called key performance indicators (KPI).

- **Communities** provides techniques to improve collaboration between users and teams. It includes the integration of Outlook, templates to set up community sites, such as blogs and wikis, as well as services that allow collaborative work on documents or tasks, including notification services.

- **Content** offers capabilities for managing content. These include those to manage paper-based documents as well as digital assets, the ability to track transactions and business records, as well as those to manage content to be published on the internet.

- **Search** provides intelligent search services. The search centers and services provided in SharePoint allow faceted search, i.e., the ability to search for different types of objects, such as persons or data. In addition, the search centers are scalable, adjustable according relevance, and support eDiscovery.

Table 2-1. Overview and innovations of SharePoint releases between 2001 and 2016

SharePoint Release	Name of Release	Elements Included in the SharePoint Wheel
2001	SharePoint Portal Server	Document Management
2003	Microsoft Office SharePoint Portal Server	Document Management, My Site
2007	Microsoft SharePoint Server	Collaboration, Portal, Search, Content Management, Business Processes & Forms
2010	Microsoft SharePoint Server	Composites, Sites, Communities, Content, Search, Insights
2013		
2016		

As with other applications, SharePoint is available under different license and provision models. However, SharePoint is not available as an open source CMS. The enterprise must always pay a fee to use the CMS. To use SharePoint 2016, two different provision models are distinguished:[4]

- **SharePoint Online** is the cloud-based version that does not operate on its own hardware. Its license model is on a per-user basis, which can be standalone or integrated as an application in Office 365, in addition to other applications, e.g., Microsoft Dynamics CRM.

- **SharePoint On-Premise** is the conventional variant not operating in the cloud, or not completely in the cloud. To use it, an enterprise must pay for the global license. The hardware to run SharePoint must be administrated by the enterprise itself or by another supplier, e.g., the Azure cloud computing service provided by Microsoft.

From a functional perspective, many different versions exist, especially for the version of SharePoint being provided online and its integration in Microsoft Office 365. The different versions differ according to the templates provided out of the box, the underlying features, and the provided SharePoint services. However, in summary, two core versions exist:

- **SharePoint Standard** is the version including only the core capabilities of SharePoint (sites, communities, content, and search). Extended techniques, such as to allow business intelligence processes, are not included. This version exists only for the on-premise one.

- **SharePoint Enterprise** is the version including the full capabilities of SharePoint (sites, communities, content, search, business solutions, business intelligence). This version allows complete ECMS processes. This version exists for both SharePoint provision models.

Core Technology

When discussing the core SharePoint technology, five main features are important. First are the hierarchies available to manage different site levels. Second are the applications made available in SharePoint to ultimately create,

---

[4]Microsoft, "SharePoint 2016 Licensing," https://products.office.com/en-us/sharepoint/sharepoint-licensing-overview, accessed March 19, 2017.

edit, and semantically structure the different types of content. Third are the technologies responsible for customizing the pages of sites on different levels. Fourth are the pages themselves, meaning the different underlying techniques to customize the site and the associated pages according to the look and feel dictated by a corporate design. Fifth is the navigation feature provided to navigate the information required. Those features are explained in detail following. A separate section presents detailed information on the templates used to create a site for a specific use case according to the needs of a firm.

SharePoint Hierarchy

In SharePoint, a fixed number of levels does not exist. This is because each installation can include various top-level sites or subordinate sites below. The sites can have subordinated subsites, and a subsite can itself have other subsites below. However, the following four types of levels are important and allow any conceivable kind of hierarchy to be built, as shown in Figure 2-1:

- **SharePoint farm** is the lowest level in the SharePoint topology. This is the installation of SharePoint performed on the selected hardware. One farm can be installed on one server or on multiple servers. However, multiple farms cannot be installed only on one server.

- **Web application** is the second-lowest level in the SharePoint topology, below the SharePoint farm. One farm can have multiple SharePoint web applications. For example, if one enterprise has two different companies, it will most likely have two web applications with two different root domains.

- **Top-level sites** are the third lowest level in the SharePoint topology, below the SharePoint web application. For each web application, multiple top-level sites can be defined. Each top-level site starts with a site collection, e.g., one site collection for the internet and another for the intranet.

- **Subsites** are the fourth-lowest level in the SharePoint typology. As the name implies, subsites are child sites of the above-mentioned site-collections. However, a subsite can also be a subsite of another subsite, subsuming the site collection, and so on. Subsites usually inherit the settings of their parent sites.

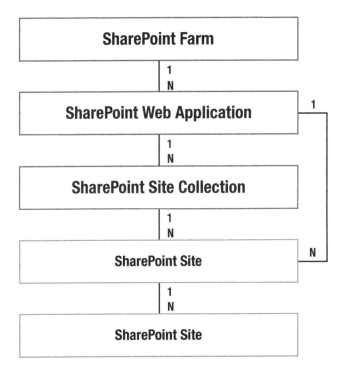

Figure 2-1. Hierarchies of different SharePoint levels for a single SharePoint farm on which SharePoint pages and SharePoint applications can be created (except SharePoint farm; note that "1" stands for a single relation, and "N" stands for multiple relations)

The contents existing on a single site, no matter the level of the site, can be controlled by using **Site Contents**. Here, the included subsites are listed, as well as the included applications. In addition, the pages being included on a site can be controlled, by using the list application known as **Pages**.

At each of the above-mentioned levels (except SharePoint farm), pages and applications can be created:

- **Applications** are the most specific level in SharePoint. Each application is a list or library structuring content, i.e., the items of a list or library. Each application provides functional features to store and manage content and information.

- **Pages** are the web sites in SharePoint. Each page is a container having static and/or dynamic content to be displayed. Each page consists of different blocks including the content. In SharePoint, these blocks are named web parts.

SharePoint Applications

An application in SharePoint is a small piece of software providing functional features to store and manage content according to type of information, i.e., a web application. In SharePoint 2016, 18 different applications exist out of the box that can be added to the level of a site collection or to the level of a SharePoint site. Additionally, applications can be added by order from the Microsoft app store. Some of the applications provided by the store are open source; for others, a fee has to be paid. Each application is of the type list, library, or calendar (also a list), whereby each type is focused on one specific type of content, namely, to store items, files, events, or tasks. The provided applications are as follows:

- **Announcements** is a list to let people know what is happening in the department, project, etc.[5] Such announcements are usually displayed on the home page of the site, but the actual storage occurs in the list mentioned.

- **Asset Library** is aimed to store all media in one place, including images, audio, or video files.[6] Through this, the media can be reused on any page. The library includes different features: thumbnail-centric view, overlay callouts, digital asset content types, and automatic metadata extraction for image files.

- **Calendar** is a list including events, very similar to the calendar provided in Microsoft Outlook. Each event can receive a title, location, start and end time, description, and category. In addition, an event can be set to be a repeating event and/or an all-day event. Different views, also similar to Outlook, exist.

- **Contacts** is a library to store contact information of other persons. Each contact can be stored in a very detailed manner. Besides the standard information, such as name, company, phone, and e-mail address, additional information, such as notes to a person, can be stored or individual columns created.

---

[5]Doug Allen, "How You Make SharePoint Announcements Grab Attention Easily Using CSR," C5 Insight Blog, www.c5insight.com/Resources/Blog/tabid/88/entryid/653/how-you-make-sharepoint-announcements-grab-attention-easily-using-csr.aspx, April 14, 2016, accessed March 19, 2017.
[6]Microsoft, "Set up an Asset Library to Store Image, Audio, or Video Files," https://support.office.com/en-us/article/Set-up-an-Asset-Library-to-store-image-audio-or-video-files-96532bf6-dc72-4f82-bf0a-21ef945c4d04, 2017.

- **Custom List** is a list of items without any predefined purpose. By contrast, the administrator, by configuring the list, as required, should define the aim of such lists. For example, a custom list can be created to store staff holidays or to list all peer companies or all sales activities.

- **Custom List in Datasheet View** is similar to the preceding, but the items on the list can be created, edited, or removed inline. In most cases, this improves usability. However, it should not be used for sensitive information, as a quick solution to edit existing items is always error-prone.

- **Discussion Board** is a list to create discussions. It is used to support communication between users. Such lists are used for exchanging experience and knowledge or to develop ideas. In SharePoint, users can reply directly in single discussions or can rate discussions and answers as best reply.

- **Document Library** is a library storing document files. It is similar to the library for storing assets, but with a focus on paper-based files. For example, Word files, Excel spreadsheets, Power Point presentations, or PDFs should be stored using this library. All files can be synced to your personal computer.

- **External List** is a list showing an external content type. External content types must be defined beforehand to be used in the discussed list. For example, an XML file outside of SharePoint can be an external content type, or a relational database of another information management system.

- **Form Library** is a library that stores forms. Such forms can be created using InfoPath, another application outside of SharePoint that creates the forms in XML format.[7] Once, the form is published inside this library, users can employ it to create and fill out InfoPath forms.

---

[7]BizSupportOnline, "What Is a SharePoint Form Library?" InfoPath Blog, www.bizsupportonline.net/blog/2014/what-is-sharepoint-form-library.htm, accessed March 19, 2017.

- **Import Spreadsheet** allows users to import data into SharePoint from an existing Excel spreadsheet. To do so, the spreadsheet should not include blank cells; representative headers should be included; and the cell formats should be consistent.[8] Please note that the input is static.

- **Issue Tracking** is a list of items performing as issues. Issues are small tasks with a priority and due date that can be assigned to persons. In addition, each issue gets a unique identifier, a title, and a status. Through this, the user can filter for active issues, as well as for issues assigned to him/her.

- **Links** is a list of items. The items can be any type of link, inside or outside SharePoint. For example, a marketing and sales department can create a list of links having interesting posts of events as link items.

- **Picture Library** is a library very similar to the library for storing assets. However, here the focus is more on storing only pictures and figures. In addition, non-print-based documents can be stored in this library, such as PowerPoint slides.

- **Promoted Links** is a list to tag artifacts as important. The tagged artifacts are afterward summarized as a specific few using tiles. It is, for example, used to provide a summary of the most important links inside an emphasized view.

- **Survey** is another list in SharePoint. It provides a quick and clear representation of answers to a survey. In addition, the resulting answers can be (automatically) analyzed using this application. The results can be graphically enhanced, and the fulfillment of the survey can be displayed.

- **Tasks** is a list in SharePoint to create, manage, and assign tasks to other users, for example, when setting up tasks for implementing a project. This list includes columns to store the creator of the task, a description of the task to be performed, the degree of fulfillment, as well as the user responsible for fulfilling this task. The tasks can be visualized using a time line, and workflows can be added to the single tasks.

---

[8]Ken Withee, "How to Import a Spreadsheet into SharePoint as an App," Dummies, www.dummies.com/software/microsoft-office/sharepoint/how-to-import-a-spreadsheet-into-sharepoint-as-an-app/, accessed March 19, 2017.

- **Wiki Page Library** is a library that includes wiki sites. Such sites are aimed to quickly capture and share ideas, by creating simple sites and interlinking different wiki sites.[9]

In addition to the above-mentioned applications, which can be created or removed by an administrator, other applications exist that can be added to the site according to the template chosen. These applications cannot be removed from the site, as they are responsible ensuring the functionality of the underlying template. Logically, the automatically included applications differ according to the aim of the template. The most important applications that are automatically created are as follows:

- **Micro Feed** is an application required in the team site to store the social interactions happening on the site. By default, the home page of the team site includes the site feed web part newsfeed. All the conversations published as feed, and the reactions of other users on it, are stored as micro feed items.

- **Style Library** is a library to store style files. Such style files can, for example, be Cascading Style Sheets (CSS) to style text stored in Hypertext Markup Language (HTML). The files stored here can be used to style master pages and page layouts in the recent site or the subsites inheriting the settings.

- **Categories** is a list to create, edit, and delete categories. Such categories are used to classify the different blog posts according to subjective or objective criteria. By default, three categories exist: events, ideas, and opinions. To share experiences, for example, such a category can be created.

- **Comments** is a list storing comments replying to an existing post. New items cannot be created in this list, and existing items cannot be edited or deleted. Through this list, each comment can be linked to the underlying post. In practice, this is often used to filter for the most interesting posts.

---

[9]Microsoft, "Create and Edit a Wiki," https://support.office.com/en-us/article/Create-and-edit-a-wiki-DC64F9C2-D1A2-44B5-AC59-B9D535551A32, accessed March 28, 2017.

- **Posts** is a list of all posts of a site. In contrast to the list storing the comments, new items can be created, and existing items can be deleted or edited. For each post, the title, the person who created the post, the publishing date, the category used to classify the post, the number of comments, and the number of likes are stored.

- **Content and Structure Reports** is a list to customize queries performing as reporting about a site collection or site. The reports are based on the physical structure of the SharePoint site.

- **Documents** is a library to store paper-based documents. The library aims to store documents used on separate pages.

- **Images** is a library to store pictures and figures. The library's aim is to store images used on separate pages.

- **Pages** is a library to store created web pages.

- **Reusable Content** is a list containing information (in HTML, or as text) that can be reused on included pages.

- **Site Collection Documents** is also a library to store documents. However, its aim is to store documents that are used throughout the complete site collection.

- **Site Collection Images** is also a library to store images. However, its purpose is to store images that are used throughout the complete site collection.

- **Workflow Tasks** is a list storing workflow tasks.

SharePoint Pages

Pages in SharePoint are web sites. Each page is a container displaying static and/or dynamic content. The pages in SharePoint are customized using two different techniques. Both are responsible for adjusting the look and feel of SharePoint, according to the needs of an enterprise. The two techniques are the following:

- **Master Page** controls the general elements of a SharePoint site, i.e., elements shown on each site. It specifies the different navigations available, the visualization of standard content (e.g., a logo), the editing modes allowed, the security levels allowed, and the allowed web parts to be used on pages.

- **Page Layout** controls the more specific elements of a SharePoint site, i.e., elements not shown on each site. Its aim is to create analogs to templates used for WCMS. Through this, a page layout includes predefined boxes and web parts tailored to the specific aim of a page.

SharePoint Web Parts

Web parts are single units of reusable components that can be employed on a SharePoint page to perform a specific task and, ultimately, to customize the pages.[10] Each web part includes specific functionality to modify the textual and graphical content, appearance, and behavior of a SharePoint page.[11] All content shown on a SharePoint page is realized using web parts. Each page includes various web part zones including web parts. The web parts can be positioned into the zones by using the browser or by using the Microsoft SharePoint Designer editor. Each web part has its own configuration menu to perform customization of the web part (see Figure 2-2). Here, the dimensions of the web part, the title of the web part, or specific functionalities, such as which content has to be queried using this web part, can be customized. Each configuration can be validated for every user or only for a recent user. In practice, web parts are often used for integrating dynamic content on a recent page—for example, to query the content of an application to appear as a summary on a recent site. SharePoint 2016 distinguishes ten of the most important types of web parts:[12]

- **Apps** web parts to display the content stored inside an application. These are required if, for example, the starting page of a site collection should provide a quick view to the newest documents, the most recent tasks, or important events.

- **Blog** web parts to display the content of a blog site. It is used if, for example, a page should summarize the most discussed blog entries, instead of having the entries isolated.

---

[10]Ashok Raja, "What Is a WebPart in SharePoint? Understanding the Basics of an Out of the Box (OTB) WebPart in SharePoint 2013" SharePoint Pals, http://sharepointpals.com/post/What-is-a-WebPart-in-SharePoint-Understanding-the-basics-of-an-Out-of-the-Box-(OTB)-WebPart-in-SharePoint-2013, January 21, 2014, accessed April 1, 2017.

[11]Microsoft, "Creating Web Parts for SharePoint," https://msdn.microsoft.com/en-us/library/ee231579.aspx, accessed April 1, 2017.

[12]Ken and Rosemarie Withee, "Common Web Parts in SharePoint 2016," Dummies, www.dummies.com/software/microsoft-office/sharepoint/common-web-parts-sharepoint-2016/, accessed March 28, 2017.

- **Business Data** web parts category specialized to display business information, such as status or other indicators. In addition, this category includes web parts to embed information from Excel and Visio documents, as well as information from external sources.

- **Community** web parts to improve community features, e.g., to display the memberships of users for groups or information about a community.

- **Content Rollup** web part to aggregate information. The aggregation is performed by searching other sites, e.g., to provide a summary of most critical tasks. Most important for this category is the Table of Contents web part.

- **Filters** web parts that are combined with other web parts (mainly search web parts). Their aim is to filter for relevant information, instead of showing the complete number of structured information inside a library or the complete items in a list.

- **Media and Content** web parts used for displaying digital assets. In SharePoint, such assets are stored in a separate application (library). The query is performed using this type of web part, as an analog to the previously mentioned web parts.

- **Project Web App** web parts that focus on administrating projects using Microsoft Project Server. The web parts can visualize specific Project Server artifacts, such as issues, tasks, time sheets, and status.

- **Search-Driven Content** web parts that allow dynamic content by using search queries. The search queries can be defined using different metadata techniques, e.g., whether a block should contain all recent items of a specific user group. Most important here is the **Content Query** web part.

- **Social Collaboration** web parts designed to display the content stored in social features of SharePoint, such as note board, tag cloud, user tasks, or contact details.

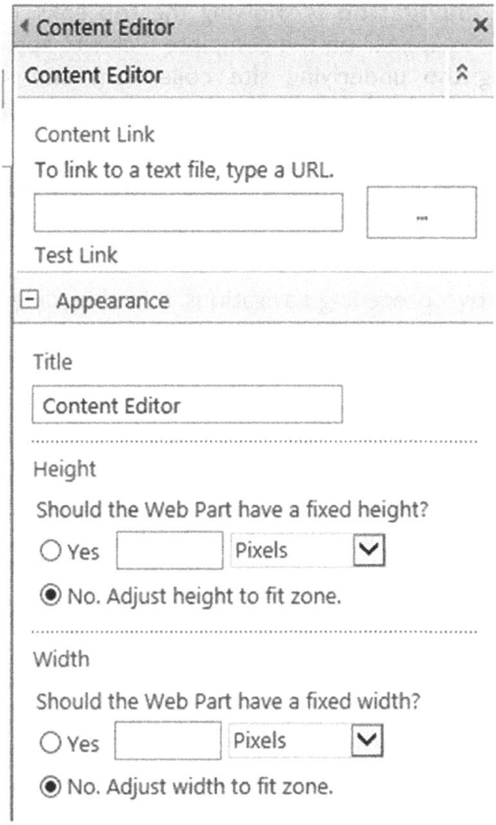

Figure 2-2. Browser user interface for editing the functionality, design, and/or behavior of SharePoint web parts

SharePoint Navigation

Navigation in SharePoint includes control elements and links on site-collection, sites, and subsites to simplify the orientation for users. Through this, users can navigate more efficiently to the content and information they actually require. In SharePoint, the navigations included on the site-collection, sites, and subsites are controlled by the underlying master page. For example, one master page includes two navigations, wherein one includes only one navigation. The navigation can finally be customized in **Navigation Settings**.

From a user's perspective, two types of navigations exist. Both can be customized according to the subsites and pages shown. The two types of navigations existing in SharePoint are the following:

- **Global Navigation** is showing the top links, meaning the links to appear on the complete web site application, including the underlying site collections and sites. It should be used for global items and very important pages.

- **Local Navigation** is showing the recent links, not the links to appear on all sites and site collections subsuming the recent site collection or web application. It should be used to show all pages of the recent site.

In addition to the two preceding navigations, a further differentiation can be made, i.e., a difference from a functional perspective. As such, two types of navigations exist:

- **Structural Navigation** is the traditional navigation. Independent of the physical structure (hierarchy) of the pages, a virtual structure can be created. With this, pages are listed by using a title to be displayed inside the navigation. The different levels of navigation can be realized by using superordinated headings. Using this traditional technique, local and global navigation can be differentiated.

- **Managed Navigation** is available since the SharePoint release presented in SharePoint 2013, a navigation realized by this technique is based on an underlying taxonomy. The term set can be edited using the **Quick Launch Bar** available directly from the shown navigation or by using the **Term Store Management Tool**. Using this metadata-driven technique, local and global navigation cannot be differentiated.

Each of the preceding navigations can be adjusted according to five criteria, namely, if the recent site should inherit the navigation of the more general site, if a managed navigation should be used for a structural navigation, if subsites and pages should be included in the navigation, and the maximum number of items in the navigation. The current navigation can, in addition, specify whether the items of the current site should be displayed only or if sibling sites should be shown as well. The structural navigation is a conventional navigation and not a formalist one. The administrator of a site can decide in a flexible manner the physical structure of the navigation, by creating a virtual one. In contrast, when using the metadata navigation, the navigation is defined by the formalism of the site collection, using its underlying taxonomy, known in SharePoint as **Term Store**.

SharePoint Master Page and Page Layouts

Master Pages control the core elements shown on SharePoint pages, such as local and global navigation, visualization of the site title, visualization of a logo, the sign-in process, ribbon, functionalities of the site, etc. **Page Layouts** control the elements to be shown in the content area and, of course, control the layout of these elements. Both master pages and page layouts can be managed by using the areas **Look and Feel** and **Web Designer Galleries** (see Figure 2-3).

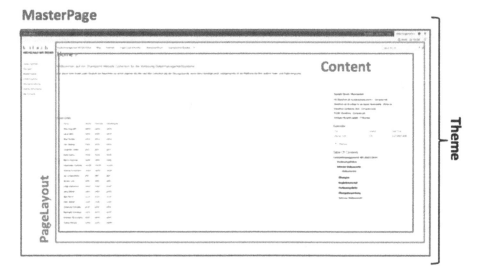

Figure 2-3. Explanation of elements and their relationships, used for realizing and customizing the look and feel of a SharePoint web application

Out of the box, two master pages are provided in SharePoint, compared in Table 2-2. A third master page exists, to be used exclusively for page development. Which master page to use can be defined in the **Site Master Page Settings**. Here, the master page used for the pages shown to every user and the master page used by administrative pages can be distinguished. It is recommended that for both types of pages, the same master page be used. The three master pages that can be used for both types of pages out of the box differ, as follows:

- **Oslo** is intended to support content rendering and to focus on the layout of the page. For this reason, it should be used in a multichannel context, i.e., for publishing on the internet.

- **Seattle** supports collaboration. This is achieved by connecting management processes provided in SharePoint. It should be used for establishing an intranet.

- **Minimal** does not have a specific aim. It is reduced to the main elements for supporting an empty master page to be used on a development basis.

Table 2-2. Overview of and differences between SharePoint master pages

Control Element	Seattle Master Page	Oslo Master Page
Navigation	Structured navigation, Local and global navigation, maximum two levels	Managed navigation, only global navigation, more than two levels possible
SharePoint Ribbon	Always visible, anonymous access not used	Invisible for anonymous users, anonymous access used
Search Slot	Automatically provided	Not provided automatically

Page layouts define how the final content should be displayed, including the underlying templates for rendering the content, and positioning the web parts and information. The page layouts provided can be managed by the **Page Layout** and **Site Template** settings. Here, the site templates have to be defined, which in turn allow choosing the included page layouts.

SharePoint Branding

Adopting the look and feel of a site according to a corporate design is known as branding. In SharePoint, branding can be quickly performed by using **Composed Looks** and its underlying **Themes**. The settings in SharePoint can be managed by using the area's **Web Design Galleries** and **Look and Feel**.

In addition to the master page, which defines the core elements to be used by the composed look, the themes feature plays a crucial role. Themes use tags to define how the elements included on a page should be displayed. There are two types of themes:

- **Color Theme** defines hex values to clarify the color used by single elements on a page, i.e., it is defined by the underlying master page. The hex values are stored in XML file format, in what are called palettes.

- **Font Theme** is analogous to the preceding but aim to define the fonts used by the elements. It's also stored as an XML file.

Composed looks are managed in the accompanying list. Here, each look is defined by five attributes: name, URL of the master page used, URL of the color theme used, URL of the background image used (optional), and the URL of the font theme. For defining which look should be used, the accompanying menu must be used. Here, different looks are listed, which can be configured by the attributes mentioned before.

For more detailed branding, the master page can be customized; the page layouts can be modified; or CSS files can be included. However, this requires that source code be developed and is much more time-consuming than the alternative presented above. Modified files can be managed by using the **Design Manager**, part of the **Look and Feel** menu. Here, the look and feel of the site in a multi-channel context, the migration of master pages, as well as the migration of page layouts, and display templates are considered. When creating such a new file, a gallery for storing snippets appears. Here, single HTML code is provided in the form of snippets representing the elements being allowed on a SharePoint page. The snippets can be used together on an individual page.

SharePoint Multilingualism

As SharePoint is often used in very large enterprises with locations in different countries, it is necessary to support multilingualism. In SharePoint, this is realized using the so-called **Multiple Language Interface** and the underlying **Language Packs**. These ensure the necessary changes to the display language of the following UI elements: web parts, site title and description, menu and actions, default columns, custom columns, navigation bar links, and managed metadata services.

The initial content is not affected by the preceding. This must be done by using Variations, which also make use of Language Packs. Variations allow the creation of different pages for the different languages.

SharePoint Pages

Pages in SharePoint are mainly used for publishing content for the web (internet, intranet, or extranet). For creating a page, different page layouts, such as article page, image left, body only, blank web part page, etc., exist. The page layouts provided on a site depend on which subsite template is actually being used. Each page to be created in SharePoint can be further defined by giving it a name, which is used to automatically create the URL of the page. All pages of site are managed by using a separate list.

Each page in SharePoint can be edited. To ensure a controlled process, the pages that are recently edited are **Checked Out**. This means, that only the person editing the page can view it. Logically, if the editing is completed, the page has to be **Checked In** accordingly, before it is finally **Published**. The editing process is further supported by providing a **Preview** of the page. When a page is edited, the editor panel appears. This reveals a status bar and a menu for performing the editing. This menu is changed according to which part, i.e., which web part, of the page is to be edited. To limit the editing process to only the necessary users, eight standard **Permission Levels** exist for SharePoint pages, with the following rights: full control, design, contribute, read, limited access, view only, approve, manage hierarchy, and restricted read. During the creation process of a page, it can adopt a different status, which can, of course, be controlled and automatized by using a workflow, more precisely, the publishing approval workflow:

- **Checked Out** means that the page has status of being edited. Only the editor is able to see a page with this status.

- **Draft** highlights that the page is stored but that editing is not complete, or that the page has already been approved but is outdated, because of it not having been published.

- **Pending** indicates that the editing is complete. However, the page requires approval before being published.

- **Approved** means that the page has been approved, and everyone having access to the page can view the page.

- **Rejected** is the opposite of the preceding status. The page is not approved and must be edited further or removed.

- **Scheduled** is another status highlighting that the page is approved. However, pages having this status are not yet published. Publication depends on a schedule.

SharePoint Search

SharePoint provides different techniques to support its search-driven applications. These aim to greatly improve the search experience for users.

The entry to a search query in SharePoint is the provided search slot (see Figure 2-4). At any time, this slot is in the same place and is accessible everywhere. The slot can query for three types of phrases: full-text search, keyword search, and person search.

Figure 2-4. Structure of the SharePoint result page, including different page elements to further help find the desired data

After typing and sending a search query, the user is forwarded to the result page. This result page includes the detected search results and provides the state-of-the-art techniques for search-driven applications:

- **Dynamic Taxonomies** are represented as search verticals. The user can further filter the results by limiting the search to a specific range or object: **Everything, Conversation, People,** and **This Site**.

- **Multilingualism** is supported. The user can filter for results expressed in a specific language.

- The results are finally presented by a **Title** and a text snippet, as well as by the place where the result is stored, i.e., its **URL**. For each result, a **Result Preview** is shown, appearing if the user hovers with a mouse over the title of the result.

- **Search Statistics** informs the user of how many relevant items are detected. If a larger number of results is detected, not fitting on a single page, **Pagination** is provided.

- Additional settings can be performed to customize the search by using **Search Preferences** or to set up a daily or weekly summary to be sent by e-mail (**Alert Me**), in the event of new results being found or existing items having changed.

- **Faceted Search** is provided to further refine the detected results. In SharePoint, this technique is named **Refiner**, which can be set up by the administrator.

The query and the result page are in SharePoint, based on a what is called a search center. Two types of search centers are distinguished. The **Basic Search Center** provides a page for showing the search results. The **Enterprise Search Center** does not look very different, except that it automatically provides the visualization of dynamic taxonomies, i.e., the search verticals. In addition, both types of search centers include an advanced search feature that has to be activated in the central administration before it can be used. This includes the other previously mentioned techniques, as well as techniques to exclude phrases, to define the language, and to define content types, illustrated in Figure 2-5.

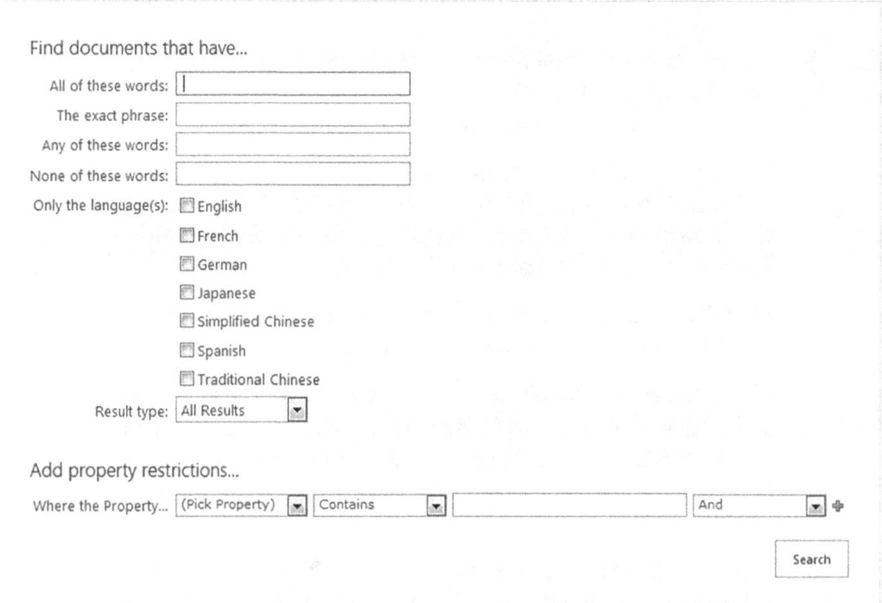

Find documents that have...

All of these words:	
The exact phrase:	
Any of these words:	
None of these words:	
Only the language(s):	☐ English
	☐ French
	☐ German
	☐ Japanese
	☐ Simplified Chinese
	☐ Spanish
	☐ Traditional Chinese
Result type:	All Results

Add property restrictions...

Where the Property... (Pick Property) | Contains | | And ➕

Search

Figure 2-5. User interface to set up advanced search features, including searches for specific words or phrases, to define the language used, set up the result type, and, finally, add property restrictions

Whether using the Enterprise Search Center or the Basic Search Center, the result page is based on the included web parts. Through this, the result page can be customized in detail, by adding further web parts or by editing existing web parts. Different web parts to improve search are provided for the following: to provide a search field for person search, to provide a field for advanced search, to provide search statistics, to summarize the search results, or to highlight the most fitting search results.

All the preceding features can be used and customized by the **Site Collection Administrator**. However, the underlying technique also has to be considered for customizing and improving the search experience. This must be performed by the more technical **Central Administrator**, inside the central administration of SharePoint, more precisely, the area named **Manage Service Applications**. Here, the administrator can analyze and monitor the crawling process, set up and tune the crawling schedule, and monitor and analyze the performed search queries.

SharePoint Authorization Concept

The authorization concept in SharePoint can be managed on different levels. This allows users to be managed precisely and to give only single users the permissions to enter the site that they actually require. Four levels exist to manage the users precisely:

- **Roles/Levels** can be assigned to SharePoint groups, or to single SharePoint users. The role is defined by the underlying permission level, which actions the user is allowed to perform on the SharePoint site, and which sites she/he can actually access.

- **SharePoint Groups** allow summarizing different users. This is very helpful, as usually not only single users have a unique level of permission.

- **Permission Levels** are assigned to the SharePoint groups or to single users (see Table 2-3). Each permission level is a collection of single types of permissions (see Table 2-4).

- **Unique Permissions** can be set up for single libraries, sites, or lists. Through this, the user or group has permission more or less to perform specific actions inside this object.

Table 2-3. Predefined permission level groups in SharePoint

Permission-Level Group	Levels of Access
Full Control	Has full control (Site Collection Administrator[s])
Design	Can view, add, update, delete, approve, and customize
Edit	Can add, edit, and delete lists; can view, add, update, and delete list items and documents
Contribute	Can view, add, update, and delete list items and documents
Read	Can view pages and list items and download documents

Table 2-4. Types of permissions in SharePoint for creating custom permission levels

Types of Permissions	Types of Level of Access
List Permissions	Manage lists, override list behaviors, add items, edit items, delete items, view items, approve items and open items, view versions, delete versions, create alerts, view application pages
Site Permissions	Manage permissions, view web analytics, date, create subsites, manage web sites, add and customized pages, apply themes and borders, apply style sheets, create groups, browse, use self-service site creation, view pages, enumerate permissions, browse user information, manage alerts, use remote interfaces, use client integration features, open and edit personal user information
Personal Permissions	Manage personal views, add/remove personal web parts, update personal web parts

In addition to the preceding, permission levels can be inherited over different site levels. For example, if a user is assigned to a group that is able to contribute to the site, and another subsite exists inheriting the permission levels, such users are also allowed to contribute to the subsite. Of course, on a subsite level, unique permission can also be created for specific objects, or the inheritance can be removed.

SharePoint Metadata Techniques

The classical features being supported inside SharePoint for managing information, e.g., documents, use folders, lists, filters, and create various views that build upon the filters. However such traditional techniques are not sufficient at present for intuitively structuring a large amount of information. Therefore, SharePoint also supports both metadata-driven techniques: folksonomies and taxonomies.

In SharePoint, taxonomies are created and managed with the **Term Store Management Tool**. Inside this tool, term sets can be created, which consist of hierarchically ordered terms. Through these, each term set depicts a taxonomy consisting of terms. Such term sets can be assigned to libraries or lists for hierarchically structuring the list items or documents. Logically, each single item or document can be assigned with one specific term.

The folksonomies are created and managed inside SharePoint using the **Enterprise Metadata** feature. In contrast to the preceding, this metadata technique does not support a hierarchical structure, as the creation of the tags is an informal one. The feature has only to be activated for lists or libraries before each user (depending on the permission level) can assign her/his own tags to the items and documents, or use existing ones.

SharePoint Workflows

In SharePoint, many **SharePoint Workflows**, which are all sequential workflows, exist out of the box. Workflows in SharePoint can be assigned to lists, items of lists, libraries, single documents of libraries, folders, and pages. Each workflow in SharePoint consists of two lists: a task list for managing the tasks to be performed within the workflow and a workflow history for controlling the current progress. In addition, for each workflow, a page exists to summarize the aforementioned lists, as well as to effectively control the recent status of the workflow. Such pages can be used to analyze bottlenecks in business processes in the form of regular reports.

Before a workflow can be initially executed in SharePoint, it has to be assigned (associated) to a list, library, document, item, or page. To do so, the user responsible to associate the workflow must have the required permission level. Of course, not every user should be allowed to associate workflows. Usually, the owners of the site or explicit users managing workflows are responsible for this. When associating a workflow, different options exist. For example, the workflow can be defined by a unique name, specific lists to administrate the workflow tasks and the workflow history can be specified, the options responsible for starting the workflow can be clarified, and how the tasks will be communicated can be addressed. In total, six different workflows exist in SharePoint out of the box, each of which has a different purpose:

- **Approval** forwards a document or item to another group or user. The group or user has the task of approving the document or item. Alternatively, they can also reject the document or item before the workflow is finished.

- **Collect Feedback** collects feedback for a document, or an item, as the name implies. This is useful when various users are part of a specific business process.

- **Collect Signatures** forwards an Office document to other users. Those users have the task of digitally assigning the sent document.

- **Three-State** tracks processes. It is used for tracking business process, such as problems, or for tracking sensitive elements.

- **Publishing Approval** is similar to the first-mentioned workflow. However, now the approval process for pages to be published on the web is considered.

- **Disposition Approval** supports data-repository and data-disposition processes. It is used for automatically removing or archiving outdated information.

My Site Technology

During the last decade, social networks have exploded. The social platforms, which are realized through Web-2.0 applications or portal systems, are used to connect with friends or for following colleagues. Some important social networks include Facebook,[13] LinkedIn,[14] and Twitter,[15] to name only a few. All provide the typical features: having a personal user profile that can be completely or partially shared with other users; possibilities for writing one's own articles in blogs, news, posts, or tweets; a contact list to link different users and automatically inform them of newsfeeds and facilitate messaging or chatting with other users.

My Site is the social network integrated into SharePoint. It provides social networking that includes a personal profile for each user, the possibility to set up newsfeeds or write one's own blog, and, of course, the ability to follow other users. With this, it combines most of the capabilities of other well-known social networks but adds the new possibility of having its own unique aim within SharePoint, namely, to strongly support collaboration, by avoiding isolated applications and documents and improving motivation. The capabilities of My Site can be quantified as two. First is My Site itself, which provides a profile to the owner in which to edit personal information and to connect with other users. Second are the features included in My Site that distinguish it from other social networks. These include the capabilities to use applications and provision of a place for managing documents in a centralized manner, instead of having them spread over different file systems and storage places.

---

[13]Facebook, www.facebook.com/, accessed June 1, 2017.
[14]LinkedIn, www.linkedin.com/, accessed April 1, 2017.
[15]Twitter. "What's Happening," https://twitter.com/?lang=en, accessed April 1, 2017.

My Site Profile

As with other social networks, each user gets his/her own user profile, i.e., her/his own My Site. The owner of the My Site can edit it, and the information can be shared with other users. Five types of information can be edited, and most of the integrated attributes and text fields can be specified according to which users can see this information (everyone or the owner; see Figure 2-6):

- **Basic Information** allows for editing general information about the My Site owner. The attribute Name can't be changed. In the text field, **About me**, the user can add a personal description. In the **Picture** attribute, the user can upload a portrait. And, in the **Ask Me About** field, the user can edit information related to her/his main area of expertise.

- **Contact Information** includes attributes to edit contact details. Here, the user can add the following contact numbers: **Mobile phone**, **Fax**, and **Home phone**. The user can also edit **Office Location**, using informal metadata (tags). In addition, the user can edit **Assistant**, using the address book.

- **Details** includes attributes to highlight the specific skills of the user and her/his experience. In the text field **Past projects**, a user can edit information about previous projects. The text field **Skills** allows for inclusion of technical or soft skills. The text fields **Schools, Birthday**, and **Interests** are geared toward more personal details about the My Site owner. All information maintained in **Details** field of the profile can be used in the global search center of SharePoint. This is important, for example, if someone does not know the name of a user but is searching for someone with specific skills.

- **Newsfeed Settings** lets the My Site owner specify what content he/she wants to follow (**Followed Tags**), how she/he should be informed (**E-mail Notifications**), if other users see friends of the user (**People I follow**), and which activities should be shown in the profile (**Activities I want to share in my newsfeed**).

- **Language and Region** allows the user to specify the language of his/her My Site, as well as its relevant time zone and region.

Basic Information **Contact Information** Details ...

Who can see this?

Work email	office-manager@shoptiexpert.onmicrosoft.com	Everyone
Mobile phone		Everyone

This number will be shown on your profile. Also, it will be used for text message (SMS) alerts.

Fax		Everyone ⬍
Home phone		Everyone ⬍
Office Location		Everyone ⬍

Enter your current location.
(e.g. China, Tokyo, West Campus)

Assistant		Everyone

Figure 2-6. Contact information, part of the My Site profile offering fields that can be edited

The Following feature of SharePoint My Site facilitates connections with other people, allowing users to follow documents, track sites, and follow tags. Following people also allows users to track their activities and detail their skills, knowledge, or recent projects. This is very helpful, for example, if a project manager is seeking prospective employees who satisfy specific requirements. Following documents allows users to know at all times what is happening to documents that are important to the owner of the My Site, e.g., if new versions have been created, workflows for management of the documents have begun, or if the document has achieved a specific workflow status. The **Following** feature is mainly used for summarizing in a centralized manner the sites the My Site owner requires. And, finally, following tags allow specific issues that are managed by using tags, e.g., keywords, to be followed. The following of people, documents, sites, and tags can be performed by searching for the objects, or searching directly on the objects themselves. For example, if the user is on a site, a button exists to activate the following of this recent site, which can in turn also be deactivated again. The activities of followed people, as well as documents, sites, and tags, can all be tracked and summarized inside the **Newsfeed** area of My Site (see Figure 2-7). Here, postings, blog entities, and the like of other users are shown, and recent activities related to sites, documents, and tags are summarized. In addition, the user can start conversations on My Site using the newsfeed area and thereby mention other persons directly.

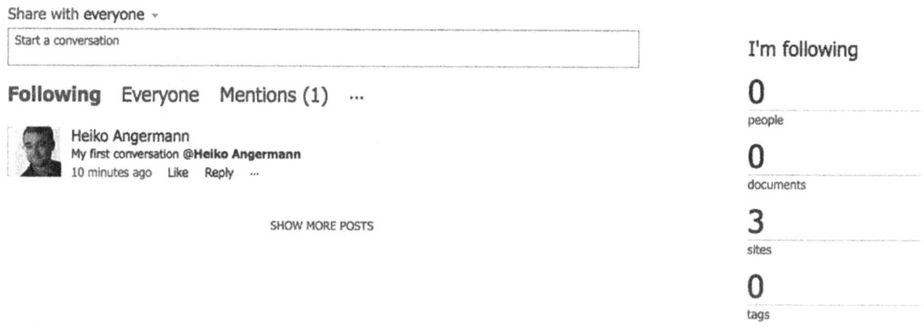

Share with **everyone** ▾

Start a conversation

I'm following

Following Everyone Mentions (1) ...

0
people

Heiko Angermann
My first conversation @**Heiko Angermann**
10 minutes ago Like Reply ...

0
documents

SHOW MORE POSTS

3
sites

0
tags

Figure 2-7. *A summary of the people, documents, sites, and tags the My Site owner can, and has been, recently following appears at the right side of the figure*

My Site Features

As with other SharePoint sites, new applications and subsites can be created in My Site (see Figure 2-8). The user can choose from applications that are also available on other sites, such as those to create a library, or of a number of subsites based on site templates, such as a site for a team or project. In practice, the application capabilities provided by My Site are often used in two types of scenarios. First, to allow users to create their own blogs, an own site template is utilized. It can be used to share with specific colleagues experiences about projects or to discuss personal topics. Second is the application for lists, which can be used, for example, to manage the addresses of contacts.

Site contents

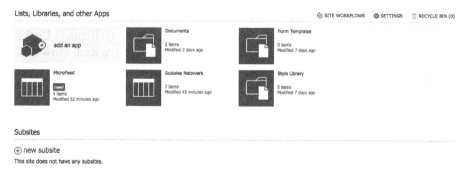

Figure 2-8. *Site contents (lists, libraries, other apps) that can be added to a SharePoint My Site out of the box*

In addition to the preceding, My Site integrates advanced document management capabilities, by giving each user his/her own central document workspace (see Figure 2-9). This can be used for uploading, creating, storing, versioning, administrating, editing, removing, and sharing any kind of document. The workspace is available using the integrated **Documents** application. This workspace is based on OneDrive, and includes document workflows (e.g., for approving documents), metadata management, as well as sharing features. Here, users can upload new documents, as provided by the documents application. The documents can be classified using folders, as provided by file directories. In addition, the documents included in the folders can be shared with other users. Other features, such as versioning and metadata features, are provided, which makes the workspace a comprehensive document management system.

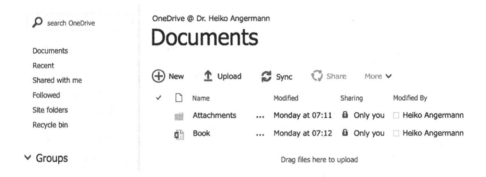

Figure 2-9. OneDrive document management interface integrated into the SharePoint My Site environment out of the box

Another My Site feature worth mentioning is the capability to manage **Links** (see Figure 2-10). Each user has an individual profile, as discussed. However, this does not only summarize the latest news from colleagues. It also provides a ribbon for managing links. With it, the user can create her/his own links to quickly navigate to the SharePoint sites required or to external links outside of SharePoint.

Figure 2-10. Managing links to be shown on the SharePoint My Site

Administration Levels

Administrating a CMS means customizing the CMS according to three requirements: technical requirements, functional requirements, and creative requirements. Technical requirements concern, for example, the relevant server farm, hardware, and the databases used to store the content. Functional requirements are that the sites fulfill the claim to support the business task, for example, to have the right template on specific sites, to have the navigation on the site as needed, to support metadata technologies used for search, but also to customize the applications according to the needs of the users. Creative requirements are mainly that the look and feel of the CMS are in the same form as on other platforms used in the form, as well as on other channels. In general, this is defined under the umbrella term corporate design (CD).

In information management systems, administration is performed in the back end. The WordPress web content management system, for example, has a back end to manage web content, and the front end is only used to visualize the content. In SharePoint, the administration must be performed differently. The reason is that the system is more comprehensive, as well as the server farm behind it. The server farm and the main functionalities, such as crawling services, have to be defined in one back-end environment, known as **Central Administration**. Here, the technical settings are found, as well as the more general functional settings. Selected users perform the customization in the front end, performing as an additional back-end section, named **Site Settings**. Here, the more site-specific functional settings are performed, as is customization. Administration in SharePoint can be performed on all topological and global levels. For example, if an enterprise uses one web application, including three site collections in which each collection has three sites, then on seven places, the administration can be performed. In addition, the settings defined for a single site can be inherited by subsites. With this, the customization must not be performed for each site, as the specification of the site above is used.

Typically, in SharePoint administration, roles are distinguished among three types, as follows[16]:

- The **SharePoint Farm Administrator** (known in Office 365 as the SharePoint Online administrator) has full access to the SharePoint farm. This administrator manages the farm completely from a technical perspective, including setting server roles, defining external content types, and creating/removing web applications or top-level sites. Logically, this administrator has access to **SharePoint Central Administration**.

---

[16]Microsoft, "About the SharePoint Online Admin Role," https://support.office.com/en-us/article/About-the-SharePoint-Online-admin-role-f08144d5-9d50-4922-8e77-4e1a27b40705, accessed March 19, 2017.

- The **SharePoint Site Collection Administrator** can be designated by the administrator explained above. This type of administrator has full access to one complete site collection. Usually, for a single site, more users are this type of administrator, but only one user is the primary site collection administrator. Of course, one person can be administrator across multiple site collections. SharePoint Site collection administrators should not have access to the farm. Their responsibilities are to give users permissions to the site collection, to manage the site collection, to manage the included pages, and to customize pages and applications.

- The **SharePoint Term Store Administrator** can be designated by the adminstrator mentioned above for a single site collection. This administrator's role is to manage the taxonomies in SharePoint to be used to manage the content with metadata.

Site (Collection) Administration

In SharePoint, the administration of site collections and sites is performed with **Site Settings**. This page includes settings to administrate the recent SharePoint site from a functional perspective. The page is automatically set up when a site or site collection is created. The page should only be accessible to users having full access to the site. Depending on the level of the site, site settings can be inherited from a more general site to a more specific site. For example, users having access to the site collection should often also have access to the children sites of the site collection. The site settings, including the main subsettings, are as follows:

- **Users and Permissions** includes pages to give users access to the sites and to manage the different types of permissions.[17] Using the **People and Groups** page, the administrator can invite users to the site. The level of access is established by using **Site Permissions**, classifying the users into groups. With this feature, existing groups can be used or new groups can be created. In addition, one page exists to define additional **Site Collection Administrators**, and one page to administrate app content.

---

[17]Microsoft, "Work with Site Settings," https://support.office.com/en-us/article/Work-with-site-settings-e94accb1-3fc8-4246-ae35-df2ed07f42f2, accessed March 18, 2017.

- **Web Designer Galleries** manages the reusable components of sites using galleries.[18] In the gallery's **Site Columns** link, columns that can be used for all lists of the site can be created. The gallery's **Site Content Type** link stores collections of columns, according to the content type. The gallery's **Master Pages** feature stores master pages and page layouts that define the general structure of the pages. The gallery's **Themes** option contains style files to change the look and feel of the site. The gallery's **Solutions** link stores customized functionalities, and the gallery's **Composed Looks** link stores themes that differ according to the master page, font, and style files.

- **Site Administration** is a section that manages various functional settings. **Regional settings** can be changed by defining the time zone, region, sort order, calendar settings, and workweek for the entire site. **Language settings** allow changes to the site through multilingual packs. User-specific text can be exported and imported using the **Export Translations and Import Translations settings**, respectively. The **Site Libraries** and Lists page lists all libraries and the lists existing on the recent site.

- **Site Collection Administration** is only included for site collections. The main focuses of this setting are to improve the search experience and the techniques employed to manage the sites of site collections having multiple hierarchical levels. The **Recycle Bin** page lists all deleted items of the complete site collection. From here, the administrator can ultimately delete the items but also restore them. The search experience can be improved by the settings **Search Result Sources, Search Result Types, Search Query Rules, Search Schema**, and **Search Settings**. In addition, two settings exist to import/export already defined search settings: **Search Configuration Import and Search Configuration Export**. The setting **Site Hierarchy** lists all subsites of the recent site collection and allows the administrator to navigate to the site settings of the subordinated sites. The **Portal Site Connection** setting is used to link one

---

[18]Ken Withee, "Web Designer Galleries in SharePoint 2013," Dummies, www.dummies. com/software/microsoft-office/sharepoint/web-designer-galleries-in-sharepoint-2013/, accessed March 18, 2017.

site collection to another site collection. **SharePoint Designer Settings** lets the administrator specify the access to this SharePoint tool.

- **Look and Feel** is a section including links to pages that affect how the site looks. Under **Title, Description, and Logo**, the title of the site and the logo can be changed. The setting **Quick Launch** is a page from which the site collection administrator can change the links of the launch. From the top page link bar, the site collection administrator can change the links of the **Top Link Bar. Tree view** is a page to additionally administrate the local navigation. Finally, **Change the Look** is a page from which the branding of the SharePoint site can be changed.

- **Site Actions** is a feature to help administrate the basic techniques of the site. The **Manage Site Features** page lets the administrator activate and deactivate features on site level. On the page **Save Site as Template**, the recent site can be saved as a SharePoint solution (template).

Central Administration

In SharePoint, **Central Administration** is the location that administrates the complete SharePoint farm, i.e., the back end of SharePoint. This type of administration is automatically set up when installing SharePoint. The tasks that can be performed here to define different types of settings require a deeper technical understanding of SharePoint. The main settings that should be administrated only by a **SharePoint Farm Administrator** are as follows[19]:

- **Application Management** allows managing the two most general hierarchical levels of SharePoint. This relates to create, edit, and remove web applications but also site collections. In addition, service applications can be managed and configured, as well as the used databases to store the content.

- **System Settings** handles the settings of used servers, messaging services, and the farm itself, including the management of services, server roles, the configuration of in-/outgoing e-mails and short messages, as well as the management of farm features and solutions and user solutions.

[19]Tutorials Point, "SharePoint—Central Administration," www.tutorialspoint.com/sharepoint/sharepoint_central_administration.htm, accessed March 22, 2017.

- **Monitoring** allows managing monitoring and reporting. Here, the **Health Analyzer** can be used to monitor the status of different services performed. In addition, **Timer Jobs** can be defined to decide when specific jobs should be issued, and reports can be created using the subsetting **Reporting**.

- **Backup and Restore** is essential to ensure the reliability of the SharePoint site. In this setting, the administrator can instruct to automatically perform regular backups, perform a manual backup, and check existing backups. Of course, the administrator can also restore the site from a backup.

- **Security** is essential to ensuring the stability of the site against attacks from inside or outside. This assurance is achieved through subsettings to administrate users, general security settings, and information policy. This includes antivirus settings, the management of blocked file types, and web part security.

- **Upgrade and Migration** is required if an upgrade from one version of SharePoint to another must performed. This is necessary if more functionalities must be supported by migrating from the standard to the enterprise version, or if a more recent version should replace an older one.

- **General Application Settings** are used to configure site collection overlapping settings. These includes **External Service Connections, SharePoint Designer settings, Search Settings and Crawler Impact Rules, Content deployment**, and **PWA settings**.

- **Apps** is utilized to manage the applications to be used in the web application. To do so, the **SharePoint and Office Store** setting is included, in which apps can be purchased and licenses of apps can be managed. In addition, the **App Management** setting controls used apps and configures the URLs of apps.

- **Office 365** is a setting available only in the on-premise version of SharePoint. The reason is that the settings here are already defined in the online version. This includes the configuration of the social-profile portal Yammer and OneDrive features.

- **Configuration Wizard** is a step-by-step wizard to semiautomatically configure a SharePoint server. It is the same wizard used when initially installing SharePoint.

As central administration in SharePoint is also a separate site, it, too, includes Site Settings, which are analogs to the site settings for site collections. The settings provided are similar to the site settings provided on the site level, as summarized in Table 2-5.

Table 2-5. Provided site settings of central administration compared to the site settings of a top-level site

Site Setting	Central Administration	Provided Settings
Users and Permissions	Completely	
Web Designer Galleries	Completely	
Site Administration	Partially	Language settings, Export Translations, Import Translations, Site libraries and lists, User alerts, RSS, Sites and workspaces, Workflow settings
Site Collection Administration	Partially	Recycle bin, Search Result Sources, Search Result Types, Search Query Rules, Search Schema, Search Settings, Search Configuration Import, Search Configuration Export, Site collection features, Site hierarchy, Site collection audit settings, Portal site connection, Storage Metrics, Site collection app permissions, SharePoint Designer Settings, HTML Field Security, Help settings
Look and Feel	Partially	Title, description, and logo, Quick launch, Top link bar, Tree view
Site Actions	Extended	Manage site features, Save site as template, Enable search configuration export, Site Collection Web Analytics reports, Site Web Analytics reports, Reset to site definition
Search	Completely	

Template Technology

In general, a template is a package that includes preconfigured properties. For publishing web sites, for example, different templates are available to simplify and standardize design and functionality. Using boxes that have a predefined style, predefined position on the page, or predefined levels of access achieve this. In SharePoint, templates also are available. However, the templates in

SharePoint do not focus on styling pages but differ in a functional perspective by including different applications and settings. The templates are available as site collection templates, which means that a top-level site is created as a child of the web application.[20] Or, similar templates can be used to create sites as part of the site collection, known as subsites. The most widely used templates are presented in this section.

Template Types

Each template is specialized to support a specific business task, by integrating the required functionalities in a starting setup. According to the license chosen, different templates are available. Some templates can be used for a site collection and subsite, others only for a site collection, as summarized in Table 2-6. Each template differs mainly from another in its predefined applications, including lists, libraries, and so forth, the site collection settings, and the predefined levels of access to the site. SharePoint 2016, as well as its predecessors, summarizes similar templates by differentiating between four distinct types[21]:

- **Collaboration Site Templates** aim to improve collaboration among users. For example, users who work together as part a team, a group of users who share ideas inside a blog, a group of developers who develop applications, a group of product owners and developers who work on projects, or a community that discusses different topics of interest.

- **Enterprise Site Templates** focus on managing sensitive content and information. Such data can be documents that are structured using semantic technologies (taxonomy, folksonomy), records to document transactions, or search centers to allow users to find the things they need at the right time.

- **Publishing Site Templates** are designed to publish information on any other type of portal. For example, the web presence of an enterprise can be published on the internet, where anonymous users can access information about the firm, or information for staff can be published on an intranet, which is not accessible to anonymous users.

---

[20]Pentalogic, "SharePoint: Top Level Site," www.pentalogic.net/sharepoint-knowledge-base/glossary/sharepoint-top-level-site, accessed March 18, 2017.
[21]Microsoft, "Default Site Templates," https://support.office.com/en-us/article/Default-site-templates-bc37dbce-7c04-4129-9769-c2790b858205, accessed March 12, 2017.

- **Custom Site Templates** are templates that are not preconfigured out of the box but are defined by the administrator of the site him-/herself. Such templates contain exactly the libraries, lists, views, and workflows, etc., that the enterprise requires for a specific task.[22] Customizing an existing template and saving it as a custom site template achieve this.

Table 2-6. Available site (collection) templates per license[23],[24]

Type	Standard/Enterprise	Availability Level	Available Templates
Collaboration	Standard	Site Collection, Site	Team Site, Blog, Project Site, Community Site
Collaboration	Standard	Site Collection	Developer Site
Enterprise	Standard	Site Collection, Site	Document Center, Records Center, Enterprise Search Center, Basic Search Center
Enterprise	Standard	Site Collection	My Site Host
Enterprise	Enterprise	Site Collection, Site	Business Intelligence Center Site
Enterprise	Enterprise	Site Collection	In-Place Hold Policy Center, eDiscovery Center, Compliance Policy Center, Community Portal
Publishing	Standard	Site Collection, Site	Enterprise Wiki
Publishing	Standard	Site Collection	Product Catalog, Publishing Portal
Publishing	Standard	Site	Publishing Site, Publishing Site with Workflow

---

[22]Microsoft, "Create and Use Site Templates," https://support.office.com/en-us/article/Create-and-use-site-templates-60371b0f-00e0-4c49-a844-34759ebdd989, accessed March 18, 2017.

[23]Microsoft, "Using Templates to Create Different Kinds of SharePoint Sites," https://support.office.com/en-us/article/Using-templates-to-create-different-kinds-of-SharePoint-sites-449eccec-ff99-4cf3-b62e-dcfee37e8da4, accessed March 20, 2017.

[24]Microsoft, "Office SharePoint 2016 List of All Sites/Web Templates," https://gallery.technet.microsoft.com/office/SharePoint-2016-Web-8548823e, accessed March 20, 2017.

Collaboration Templates

The collaboration templates are designed to improve collaboration among users working together in any way. In SharePoint 2016, the following collaboration templates, with their different scopes, are available:

- **Team Site** is a place where a group of users can work together. In practice, this template is usually used to represent a static group, illustrated inside an organization as a department, or as a more general sector. However, it can also be used to represent a dynamic team with users in different departments or sectors.

- **Blog** is a site template allowing users to quickly share and discuss any topic of interest. For example, it allows users to post ideas or observations and to share expertise. In addition, a blog allows various users to contribute to the posts of others, for example, by leaving a comment.

- **Developer Site** is a site for developers working on applications for Office. This site makes it easier to create, test, deploy, and publish apps. It can be used to manage the creation of small development projects. For larger development projects, more comprehensive tools should be used.

- **Project Site** is a site for processing smaller projects. In enterprises, it is used to store project documents, milestones, status, and communications in one place. For larger projects, other applications should be used, e.g., Microsoft Project Server or Microsoft Team Foundation Server.

- **Community Site** is a place to discuss topics of common interest. It provides different filters and metadata features that allow users to see the most relevant posts, categorize posts, or rate posts. As such, it is similar to the template for managing a blog, but with more comprehensive features.

Team Site

The Team Site template is one of the most famous templates in SharePoint. It is aimed to improve collaboration and knowledge exchange by connecting a group of users to the information, content, and applications they rely on daily.[25]

---

[25]Microsoft, "What Is a SharePoint Team Site?" https://support.office.com/en-us/article/What-is-a-SharePoint-team-site-75545757-36c3-46a7-beed-0aaa74f0401e, accessed March 14, 2017.

The group of users having access to a team site can be more or less fine-grained. For example, each sector of a firm can have its own site for a team; each department can have its own site; or each group with an even more specialized focus can have a separate site. Naturally, users can also be members of different such sites. For example, a user can be in an *Inside Sales* site for a team, collaborating with her/his direct team, but also in a *Marketing and Sales* site for another team, wherein the users of *Inside Sales* and the users of *Key-Account Management* can also collaborate.

To improve collaboration between users having access to such a site, the template includes by default the following applications: site pages, documents, and site assets. In addition, two mandatory applications are provided allowing the functionality of this template: micro feed and style library.

Blog Site

By using the Blog Site template, a site is created to quickly discuss topics in posts. In practice, the topics discussed in blogs are vary greatly. For example, a product of the firm can be discussed in a blog.

The home page of a site collection using this collaboration template lists all published posts. Additionally, it shows different blog tools to lead the user to the accompanying function. The **Create a post** function navigates a current user to the list to create a new post item. Manage posts navigates a current user to the list to manage the different existing posts. Manage comments navigates a recent user to the list to manage the different comments, i.e., a reply to an existing post. Manage categories navigates a user to the list storing all categories. Such categories are used to classify the posts according their content. **Change post layout** specifies how the summary of the posts on the home page should look like. Three different layouts are provided out of the box: basic, boxed, inline.

To facilitate quick discussion of any topic, the Blog Site template includes the following standard applications: photos and four mandatory applications are used to support the administration of different blog posts: categories, comments, posts, and style library.

Project Site

By using the Project Site template, a site is created to manage projects. From the technical side, this template is very similar to the team site template but includes additional features to focus on a dynamic team.

The home page of a site collection or site using this template gives a summary of the project using the **Project Summary** web part. Here, tasks provided by the tasks application can be included. For example, this web part can be customized to show all project members the tasks in progress or the most important deadlines. The home page also displays recent news inside a web part, showing the newsfeed. Inside this web part, users can start new conversations. For example, if a software developer has a question for the product owner about the requirements of a module, she/he can create a conversation using this web part. In addition, the home page using this template lists relevant documents. The documents are provided via the documents application. In the end, the template includes some of the functionalities provided by other project management tools, such as Microsoft Project Server, or provided by issue tracking systems like Atlassian Jira.[26] The template can be used to manage smaller projects or projects with less agility. For larger projects and agile software development projects, the aforementioned systems should be used.

The included applications are as follows: site assets, tasks, calendar, micro feed, and style library.

Enterprise Templates

Enterprise templates aim to provide sites for aggregating, analyzing, and finding content. In SharePoint 2016, the following enterprise templates, with their different scopes, are available:

- **Document Center** is a site to manage documents, including paper-based documents and assets. It provides the same features as standalone DMS.

- **In-Place Hold Policy Center** is a site to manage business or compliance regulations.[27] By using this template, an enterprise can manage policies to preserve content for a fixed period.

- **eDiscovery Center** is a template to create sites to manage the preservation, search, and export of content for legal matters and investigations.

- **Records Center** is a site to help enterprises control the management of records. It provides the same features as a standalone ERMS.

---

[26]Atlassian, "JIRA Software," www.atlassian.com/software/jira, accessed March 28, 2017.
[27]Microsoft, "Overview of in-Place Hold in SharePoint Server 2016," https://support.office.com/en-us/article/Overview-of-in-place-hold-in-SharePoint-Server-2016-5e400d68-cd51-444a-8fe6-e4df1d20aa95, accessed March 12, 2017.

- **Compliance Policy Center** is a site to manage policies to delete documents after a specified period of time. Such policies can be used over specific site collections and templates.

- **Enterprise Search Center** is a search center covering the entire enterprise. It provides faceted search and can be customized according to search queries and relevance.

- **My Site Host** is a site on which to host My Sites. Through My Site, each user can have a personal page. Such personal pages perform like well-known social media pages.

- **Community Portal** is a site to list all community sites in one directory.[28] It allows users to find the community that most fits their interests.

- **Basic Search Center** is similar to the **Enterprise Search Center** but without faceted search and with fewer customization capabilities. Additionally, it will not appear in site navigation.

Document Center Site

The Document Center Site is a SharePoint site collection and site template for managing documents at the enterprise level, as provided by a DMS.

In contrast to the SharePoint **Documents** application, the template should be used autarchically. This means that the application can be included as one performing in parallel to other applications, but the template should be used only to manage documents, i.e., different types of documents. The home page of a site collection using this template gives a list of the newest documents and a list of the recent documents modified by the recent user. Both lists are web parts performing on the underlying applications. To effectively manage the documents, five techniques are most important.[29] First is the integration of the **Managed Metadata** service to formally classify each document (taxonomy) and to use the categorization for navigation. Second is the Documents **IDs service** to classify each document with a unique identifier. Third is

---

[28]Microsoft, "Create a Community Portal," https://support.office.com/en-us/article/Create-a-community-portal-e08d0f50-05dc-4888-aa27-60ccf8f32ded, accessed March 12, 2017.
[29]Microsoft, "Use a Document Center Site," https://support.office.com/en-us/article/Use-a-Document-Center-site-06096070-d83f-45b8-b02d-ec7a4cf85cac, accessed April 1, 2017.

Document Versioning included to create a unique version for each step of the document. And fourth is the included **Content Types** service, which enables a document to be specified automatically to the appropriate setting.

In total, eight applications are included to manage the different types of contents, as well as to support the previously mentioned services: documents, site collection documents, style library, workflow tasks, content and structure reports, reusable content, site collection images, tasks.

Business Intelligence Center Site

The Business Intelligence Center Site is a SharePoint site to store, administrate, and visualize business intelligence (BI) content.[30] BI content is used in enterprises to analyze data and support decision making.[31]

BI Center sites have different characteristics than most other templates. The reason for this is that the focus of such a site is not a single application but the techniques to enable BI. In SharePoint, the capabilities of BI are achieved by using mainly four features.[32] First, BI center provides prebuilt lists and libraries for BI content, to improve the organization and usage of BI content. The main libraries/lists are the **Dashboard** library, which stores related reports; the **Data Connections** library, used for data from outside SharePoint; the **Documents** library, to store, for example, Excel spreadsheets that are used in dashboards, and the **Pages** library, containing a list of pages stored by the BI Center. Second, **Performance Point Services** content ultimately creates the BI reports, scorecards, and dashboards to support decision making. Third, the service named **Sample files** is used to support users unfamiliar with the subject of BI. Here, files, including dashboards, spreadsheets, etc., can be used to familiarize users with BI. Fourth is the **Links** service, which offers helpful information about BI tools and has a similar aim as the preceding BI center site component.

Search Center Sites

Search Center Sites help users to quickly find the content and information they specifically require. This is a very important task, as in our digital era, the amount of content is rapidly increasing.

---

[30]Microsoft, "What Is a Business Intelligence Center?," https://support.office.com/en-us/article/What-is-a-Business-Intelligence-Center-dcd208d0-f50b-46fb-ac8a-3c9a8b2ab357, accessed March 21, 2017.
[31]Gartner, "Business Intelligence," Gartner IT Glossary, www.gartner.com/it-glossary/business-intelligence-bi/, accessed March 21, 2017.
[32]Ibid.

In SharePoint, the search centers are a central site from which to perform search queries. The types of searches that can be performed in SharePoint are full-text search, keyword-based search, and person search. The presentation of the search results in the search center sites is also manifold. The results can be additionally reduced, using facets performing as filters. The results are additionally displayed, not only by the name, but by using the format symbol, the data title, a snippet highlighting the first text of, for example, a document, and by using its URL to show the storage location. Pagination is shown if the results do not fit on one page. In addition, a result statistic is shown, displaying the number of detected results. Apart from the intelligent filters and the manifold visualization, the user can create a search agent and can define search preferences. In the search agent, the user can specify queries. If a new content or information is available satisfying the query, the user is automatically informed.

In SharePoint, two templates exist to support search. The **Basic Search Center**, on the one hand, and the **Enterprise Search Center**, on the other. The latter template includes all functionalities of the other search center but also additional predefined filters, as follows: **Everything**, to get results for any type of content; **People**, to restrict results only to persons; **Conversations**; and **Videos**. New filters can also be created with this template. Both templates also include a technology named **Advanced Search**. It allows users to designate filters, word fragments to be included, word fragments to be excluded, the definition of the used language, and the specification of new content types.

Publishing Templates

Publishing templates provide sites creating, modifying, and, finally, publishing content on an intranet or the Internet.[33] In SharePoint 2016, the following publishing templates are available:

- **Publishing Portal** (or **Publishing Site**, as a site template) is a site to manage publishing content intended for the web. Publishing can be performed on the Internet (anonymous access) or an intranet (restricted access).

- **Enterprise Wiki** is a site to manage knowledge. In enterprises, wikis allow knowledge sharing by the staff inside the system, instead of having the knowledge decentralized.

- **Product Catalog** is a site that allows the administration of product-related content. It provides the same features as standalone Product Information Management (PIM) systems.

---

[33]Microsoft, "About Publishing-Enabled Site Templates," https://support.office.com/en-us/article/About-publishing-enabled-site-templates-b4fa3dcd-f4cc-4820-aa73-fed106965725, accessed April 1, 2017.

Publishing Portal

The Publishing Site template, and the site collection template known as Publishing Portal, is a place to publish web-based content, as provided by a WCMS. This content can be published on an extranet, an intranet, or on the Internet, either for selected or anonymous users. An overview of some Internet presences realized with SharePoint can be found on the SharePoint demo site.[34]

At the site level, two different templates exist. First is the **Publishing Site** template, which does not include the capability to use workflows. However, such a capability can be activated as site collection feature. Second is the **Publishing Site**, which has an existing active workflows feature. Workflows are necessary, if the publishing process requires an approval process. For publishing web-based content, four features are crucial and covered in the SharePoint Publishing template. First, templates must be available, to quickly design the web pages. This is achieved in SharePoint by using master pages, which is responsible for structuring the main content of the web pages, and through Page Layouts, which defines the position of different attributes. Second, the web pages must be organized hierarchically, for example, whether one page is a child page of another page. This is achieved in SharePoint through different navigation features, such as **Quick launch** and/or **Tree View**. The third feature concerns the usage of workflows, if the web page must be approved before publishing. In SharePoint, this is achieved through approval workflows. Fourth, the web pages should not only contain static information, if information is reused often on multiple web pages. This is achieved in SharePoint through web parts. Web parts exist to query content and to show the queried content.

In the SharePoint publishing portal/site template, the above-mentioned requirements are supported by the following applications: content and structure reports, documents, images, pages, reusable content, and site collection documents. Most important is the Pages application, as it is listing all pages with its accompanying status. In Site Settings, the most important areas are: web designer galleries, for administrating the layouts, as well as look and feel, to customize the branding of SharePoint.

.

---

[34]Microsoft, "SharePoint Internet Sites—Adapted," accessed April 1, 2017, http://www.spsdemo.com/websites/Lists/OldList/DispForm.aspx?ID=3021&Source=http%3A%2F%2Fwww%2Espsdemo%2Ecom%2Fwebsites%2FLists%2FOldList%2FAllItems%2Easpx%23InplviewHash2ceb745a%2D593c%2D428e%2Daf87%2DDee0fd405d2c3%3DFilterField1%253DPlatform%2DFilterValue1%253DSPS%2525202013&ContentTypeId=0x0100660CF76371114F2AB72BD63111D9045801003125B87E565D5F45BA4AE7B707AF766F00F37F93FC79908D498AECFC3A280E1FDA.

Enterprise Wiki

The Enterprise Wiki is a place to share knowledge. For example, the experience about a product, or documentation about a module developed or purchased, can be stored as a wiki entry inside a wiki portal.

For wiki portals, three requirements are crucial. First, the wiki portal should improve the communication of information (knowledge). This is achieved when too many communications are considered in the wiki portal. Second, the wiki portal should improve the exchange of information. This is achieved through techniques enabling to share wiki entries with other users. Third, the search ability of information should be improved to help users quickly find the wiki entry required. This is achieved through formal metadata (tags). Such tags allow the creator, but often also the readers, of the wiki entry to describe the content of the entry in his or her own words, on the one side. On the other side, the tags help other users, but also the user that created the tags, to quickly find or recover the wikis desired through using multiple tags as a query.

The above-mentioned requirements are satisfied using the interlinking between multiple applications. In addition, other applications are included that allow the use of figures in wiki entries or automatize entries using workflows: content and structure reports, documents, images, pages, reusable content, site collection documents, site collection images, style library, and workflow tasks.

Product Catalog

The Product Catalog template is a cross-site feature in SharePoint. It provides the same functionalities as a product information management system, i.e., a system to semantically structure products.

In SharePoint, and in general, cross-site means that the content is stored in one database (system) but can be published on multiple devices and channels. Typical cross-site scenarios are referred to as multichannel, cross-media (or cross-channel), and omni-channel, depending on the interaction between the channels and devices. As such, the **Product Catalog** in SharePoint is not a typical template focusing on specific applications, as it is more an architectural template focusing on allowing different types of cross-site use cases and the semantic storage of products. To provide cross-site scenarios and different types of metadata techniques, different techniques are considered in this SharePoint template. This is mainly achieved through three web parts that aim to dynamically search for the products stored on this site and taxonomy technologies.[35] The **Content Search Web Part** allows users to build their own content search queries. An example of this is a product that includes different text attributes (e.g., title, short description, long description, article information) but for which not every description should be displayed on the published web site (e.g., the query *product text* should only contain a title and short description). The **Search Results Web Part** is the counterpart to the preceding web part. Essentially, it allows to finally publish the searched content on the web site. For example, the search query *product text* is defined once but should be used on the web site summarizing all products and on the site showing only the recent product with additional queries. The **Managed Metadata Service** (also referred as **Term Store**) is the most important technique of the template to semantically structure the products and to ultimately find them.

The managed metadata service in SharePoint provides **Managed Metadata Navigation** and **Faceted Navigation** links. The first uses the taxonomic structure stored as **Term Store** as local or global navigation on the site. The latter uses the taxonomic structure also stored as term store to show so-called facets on the site. Facets are contextual refiners for the single terms.

Conclusion

This chapter reviewed the SharePoint technology of Microsoft's most recent release, SharePoint Server 2016, as well as the technology of its templates. First, the basic elements of the recent release were explained, including a comparison with previous releases. Additionally, a comprehensive discussion of the core technologies of SharePoint was presented. Afterward, the core element of SharePoint for improving collaboration was discussed, namely, the My Site technology. Preceding that was a discussion of the different levels of administration. Next, the various types of templates were explained in detail. The underlying ideas behind collaboration, enterprise, and publishing templates were discussed, as were the different types of templates that can be used in real-world business cases.

---

[35]Benjamin Niaulin, "What Is the SharePoint Product Catalog and Do I Need It?" Sharegate, https://en.share-gate.com/blog/migrate-sharepoint-2013-what-is-product-catalog, accessed March 21, 2017.

Hands-On Tutorials

This chapter offers practical experience of the core capabilities of the SharePoint enterprise content management system. It includes various tutorials concerning the main technologies of SharePoint, on the one hand, and the most-widely used techniques required in most use cases, on the other. The aim of the tutorials is mainly to increase the learning process, not only about the technologies covered in the second chapter, but also to prepare readers for the best practices presented in the fourth chapter. The tutorials presented in this chapter are all based on real-world requirements. Thus, a fictitious firm is featured that is nonetheless quite similar to one in the real-world. The fictive firm is based on a software service provider located in Germany that has almost 25 members. Of course, the firm has different departments as well as different roles. This allows simulation of the most widely applied functionalities available with SharePoint.

The focus of the tutorials is principally on seven main SharePoint capabilities, which translate into seven tutorials. Each successive tutorial increases in complexity, and each includes exercises that must be performed by the reader (user). Again, the complexity of the exercises increases with each exercise. All the tutorials and included exercises are aimed at readers who have little or no experience with SharePoint. Because of this, the focus of the tutorials is on readers who have never customized

© Heiko Angermann 2017
H. Angermann, *Manager's Guide to SharePoint Server 2016*,
https://doi.org/10.1007/978-1-4842-3045-9_3

a SharePoint site before. Depending on the complexity of the exercise, greater or less detailed explanations are provided. After completing all the tutorials and exercises, the reader will be able to understand the core SharePoint responsibilities. Of course, the reader will not be able to perform all tasks as performed by a site or site collection administrator, who is typically responsible for customizing a site. However, the reader will get an idea of what an administrator has to do to improve the usability of the application according to an enterprise's needs. In addition, she/he will experience a methodical progress, meaning that the reader will be able to imagine how SharePoint works and how it can help improve a firm's chances of success through its core capabilities. Through this, the reader will acquire an idea for which types of her/his business tasks she/he could use which type of SharePoint technology. In the end, the focuses of the tutorials are as follows:

- **Permissions** are discussed to experience SharePoint's possibilities for managing different users with different roles inside the firm. As such, tutorials including exercises to treat permissions are required for the later tutorials, because they treat the different permission levels available in SharePoint and the different user groups required to assume different roles across an enterprise.

- **My Site** is discussed so that readers can experience SharePoint's possibilities for improving social networking. Readers will be able to better understand what My Site is and how it can be used to improve communication between staff, to more quickly share information with others, and have a place for each user to collect news, discuss topics, etc.

- **Look and Feel** is elaborated, so that the readers will experience how they can quickly adapt the SharePoint site according to the needs of their firms. This includes techniques to use the already existing themes, to change information about the site, as well as techniques to integrate personal styles into the SharePoint site.

- **Applications** is discussed, because it will help readers to better distinguish between the different types of applications and to determine when to use one of these types. In addition, readers will experience which possibilities exist, to extend, and also to customize the lists and libraries created.

- **Enterprise Metadata** and **Managed Metadata** tutorials will help the readers experience how they can integrate metadata techniques into SharePoint applications. In addition, readers will consider how both techniques differ and, of course, which benefits both types of metadata technologies have in real-world scenarios.

- **Search Center** is discussed, as finding the desired information quickly is a crucial factor in our digital age, the tutorials presented on this subject focus on integrating a search center template into SharePoint. In addition, different techniques are discussed to customize the SharePoint Search Center according to the needs of a specific firm.

- **Tasks** are the scope of another type of tutorial presented. These tutorials focus on how to quickly set up one's own project workspace. This includes exercises to create new task items in SharePoint and how to nest different tasks as subtasks. In addition, exercises are included to assign tasks to different users and to administrate the project time line.

The remainder of this chapter is organized as follows. The first section starts by detailing the fictitious firm. In the second section, the technical preparations to be able to perform the tutorials are explained. In the third section, seven tutorials are presented. The tutorials explore how to manage different types of users inside SharePoint, how to improve social networking using SharePoint, how to customize the SharePoint look and feel, how to use and customize SharePoint applications, how to integrate enterprise and managed metadata technologies, how to set up and adapt the SharePoint search center, and how to administrate and manage tasks of projects.

Tutorials Methodology and Preparation

The tutorials presented in the next section, are based on a fictitious firm called ShoptiExperts, a software service provider located in Germany. We'll assume that ShoptiExperts was founded in 2005 and has a staff of 20. In addition, let's assume that two external partners exist, who are mainly provided to highlight strategic questions.

The main goal of ShoptiExperts is to implement and optimize e-commerce solutions in a B2B (business-to-business) context. The focus of the firm is on front-end design and modules to be used in the e-commerce system, named Shophouse.[1] Because ShoptiExperts wants to improve internal processes, the company has decided to use SharePoint. In the section at hand, the firm is presented in detail, that is, the expectations the company has of its systems are explained. In addition, the preparations required to perform the tutorials are also explained.

---

[1] Fictivious e-commerce system.

Tutorials Methodology (Fictitious Firm)

In the past, ShoptiExperts had used only a web content management system (WCMS) to organize its online presence. The WCMS was isolated from other information. The information and content to be used by employees was mainly dispersed over different file directories, mails, or made available as printed documents. Overall, all members of staff had problems finding the information they required, and, often, the information was uniquely in the head of a single employee instead of being available in a system. Those are the reasons the firm has decided to invest in an enterprise content management system (ECMS). Through using such a system, the firm expects to improve the effectiveness of the employees. The main focuses in the selection of an ECMS were on effectively managing users, having possibilities to improve social networking, having a system able to be customized in terms of its look and feel, integrating easily applications similar to the handling provided by Office products, having a system capable of using metadata techniques to help find information, having a system providing an improved search experience to quickly create and manage a project, and automatizing some of the daily business tasks by using workflows. Finally, the firm decided to use SharePoint, as it covers all those criteria. The firm elected to use the standard on-premise version of SharePoint 2016. At a later date, the firm will consider using Microsoft's SharePoint Online.

Depending on the responsibilities, leadership, and productivity, the employees have different roles. In total, five roles exist (see Figure 3-1).

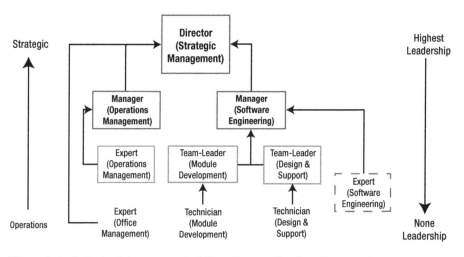

Figure 3-1. Roles (and departments) of ShoptiExperts (bordered boxes indicate leading roles: red = highest level; blue = second level; green = third level; dashed blue = representative)

Across all departments, ShoptiExperts has a total of 22 employees (see Table 3-1 and Table 3-2):

- **Director** is the paramount role, subordinate to no other. This role assumes the most leadership responsibility and has no direct influence on daily business tasks.

- **Manager** is the role subordinate only to that of the director. Managers have strong leadership responsibilities but lesser influence on direct productivity, except during escalation phases.

- **Team leader** is the role subordinate to that of the manager of the software engineering department. The leadership is low, but their influence on daily tasks is strong.

- **Expert** is a position without any management responsibilities. Power and influence depend on the power of the department an employee is a permanent member of.

- **Technician** is another role having no management responsibilities. Their tasks include developing modules and front-end design.

Table 3-1. *Permanent members of staff of the software service provider of ShoptiExperts*

Nr.	First Name	Last Name	Department	Role	Representative
1	Strategic	Director	Strategic Management	Director	2
2	Operative	Manager	Operative Management	Manager	3
3	Operative	Expert1	Operative Management	Expert	4, 5
4	Operative	Expert2	Operative Management	Expert	3, 5
5	Operative	Expert3	Operative Management	Expert	3, 4
6	Office	Expert1	Office Management	Expert	7
7	Office	Expert2	Office Management	Expert	6
8	Software	Manager	Software Engineering	Manager	9
9	Software	Expert	Software Engineering	Expert	8
10	Design	Leader	Design & Support	Team-Leader	11
11	Design	Technician1	Design & Support	Technician	12, 13
12	Design	Technician2	Design & Support	Technician	11, 13
13	Design	Technician3	Design & Support	Technician	11, 12
14	Design	Technician4	Design & Support	Technician	15

(continued)

Table 3-1. (*continued*)

Nr.	First Name	Last Name	Department	Role	Representative
15	Design	Technician5	Design & Support	Technician	14
16	Module	Leader	Module Development	Team-Leader	17
17	Module	Technician1	Module Development	Technician	18
18	Module	Technician2	Module Development	Technician	17
19	Module	Technician3	Module Development	Technician	20
20	Module	Technician4	Module Development	Technician	19

Table 3-2. Silent partners of the software service provider of ShoptiExperts

Nr.	First Name	Last Name	Department	Role	Representative
21	External	Director1	Strategic Management	Director	-
22	External	Director2	Strategic Management	Director	-

Each employee is a member of one in a total of six permanent departments. The departments are classified into three hierarchical levels, including sub and superordinate departments:

- **Strategic management** is the top-level department of the firm having no superordinate department. The main responsibility of this department is the acquisition of projects and clients, as well as key-account management. In addition, the development of hiring plans and the recruitment of staff, depending on new strategies, is among its main responsibilities. Only directors belong to this department.

- **Operations management** is the department subordinating the department explained above. In contrast to the latter, it controls business processes on a daily basis. The main responsibility is product ownership. In addition, customer service and support during the project phase are among its main responsibilities. The department is made up of a manager, who leads the department, and a group of experts.

- **Office management** is another department subordinate to the strategic management department. Its intervention power is limited, as its focus is on supporting the two aforementioned departments. Its main responsibility is to issue invoices to clients. The director (of strategic management) directly manages the experts of this department.

- **Software engineering** is also subordinate to strategic management. However, its focus is not on administration. It manages the software developers and intervenes if development processes are disturbed. In addition, the team provides technical consulting before and during the project phase. One assistant (expert) supports the manager.

- **Design and support** is a department subordinate to the software engineering department. Its main responsibility is to develop templates to be used by the Shophouse e-commerce system arm of the company. Logically, another responsibility is the adaptation of templates used by the Shophouse. A team leader, who assigns tasks to template experts, manages this team. In addition, the team leader is also involved in processing issues.

- **Module development** is another department subordinate to the software engineering department. The main responsibilities of this department are the development of modules to be used in the Shophouse e-commerce system. Another responsibility is the development of data interfaces interacting with the database used by the Shophouse. A team leader, who assigns tasks to module experts, manages this team. In addition, the team leader is also involved in processing issues.

Tutorials Preparation

To take the tutorials presented in the following sections, it is necessary to have access to a SharePoint application and to create users.

If no access is already provided to a SharePoint environment, SharePoint can be installed locally by using on-premise version of SharePoint. To install SharePoint locally, SharePoint must be downloaded, and the Windows Server 2012 R2 or Windows Server 2016 operating systems must be installed on your personal computer or virtual machine. A complete explanation of the install instructions can be accessed directly from the relevant Microsoft page.[2] In addition, a very comprehensive video provided to the public explains the complete process in great detail.[3] As a detailed explanation of SharePoint

---

[2]Microsoft, "SharePoint Server 2016," Download Center, www.microsoft.com/en-us/download/details.aspx?id=51493, accessed April 29, 2017.
[3]YouTube, *SharePoint 2016 Standalone Installation (Single Server Farm)—Full Video*, sharepointtemplates, www.youtube.com/watch?v=fABPhjGU-VY, May 23, 2016, accessed April 29, 2017.

Server 2016 is not within the purview of this book, I refer the reader to the recommended video.

As an alternative to the preceding, and recommended for starting the tutorials quickly, a trial version of Office 365 can be used. A trial version includes the online version of SharePoin. Both possibilities include the same functionalities required to perform the tutorials and the corresponding exercises. Office 365 is a cloud service provided by Microsoft. In addition to other useful applications, such as Outlook, Excel Online, PowerPoint Online, etc., it includes SharePoint. Through this, no installation of SharePoint is required in order to gain access to a SharePoint platform. Only an e-mail address must be provided. Depending on the type of mail address, the trial expires after one month (personal mail), or after three months (professional mail). One thing to be critically considered is that the SharePoint provided inside Office 365 provides another user interface as the on-premise version, known as the modern interface. To overcome this, the user must choose *Return to classic SharePoint*, when prompted. After doing this, the look and feel of SharePoint is the same as those provided by SharePoint On-Premise.

The firm presented in Tables 3-1 and 3-2 consists of 22 users. There is really no need to create an account for every user. For the two managers, at least, an account should be created, to allow for the purpose of demonstrating minimal collaboration. The creation of a 22-user account (or of two user accounts) can be performed by importing Active Directory (AD) or by using AD manually. To do so, for each member of staff, a last name and first name must be specified, using Table 3-1 and 3-2 as guides. In addition, for each user, a login name must be specified, as well as a password. Using SharePoint Online, users can be created using the user interface, or through an AD importer.

▓ **Note** For all the tutorials presented in the following section, the reader is assumed to be the employee named Operation Manager, with full access to all SharePoint features.

Hands-On Tutorials and Their Use Cases

The tutorials presented in this section are designed to provide readers with practical experience with the core capabilities of SharePoint 2016. Specifically, this section includes tutorials concerning the main technologies of SharePoint, and through these, it covers the most widely used techniques required. The tutorials aim mainly to increase the learning process with regard to the technologies outlined in the second chapter and to prepare the reader for the best practices and more detailed technologies presented in the fourth chapter.

In total, seven tutorials are offered in this section. A tutorial relates to a specific goal that an enterprise has. The goals presented as tutorials are to set up user management, improve social networking, customize the look and feel of a site, integrate applications, use metadata techniques, improve search experience, and manage tasks. To better distinguish between milestones ultimately required to satisfy a tutorial's goal, different use cases are included in each tutorial. For example, the goal of the tutorial to improve social networking includes two milestones (use cases). The first milestone (use case) is to maintain the My Site profile. The second milestone (use case) is to use My Site features. Each milestone can be considered independently, but both milestones (use cases) are required to satisfy the goal of the tutorial. Finally, as each milestone requires different steps to be performed, these are treated as single exercises. Through this, each main technique being required to be completed in SharePoint is considered independently. This has the benefit of allowing a success control to be performed after each main step and that not too many different requirements are mixed. For example, the milestone (use case) to use My Site features includes three exercises to treat three main steps: to create a blog, manage documents, and customize links. After each exercise has been performed, the milestone (use case) is finally completed. Note that the solutions presented in the fifth chapter follow the same conventions.

Note   Solutions to the tutorials can be found in the fifth chapter. For all tutorials, the goal is to explain the main techniques necessary to perform the related exercises. Each exercise can include practical components and/or functional questions. Depending on the complexity of the exercises, either the main steps involved in performing the exercise are presented or complete steps are provided. It is assumed that the tutorials will be performed in consecutive order. Because of this, not every step is repeatedly explained, as it already has been in a previous tutorial. Please also note that important steps to be performed inside SharePoint are highlighted in *italic*. The same for natural words, those are also highlighted in *italic*. To better find the main techniques to be used in SharePoint, the techniques are written as provided in SharePoint, normaly starting with an upper case letter (e.g. *Site Settings*).

Tutorial 1: User Management

The SharePoint user management is available in *Site Settings* and the included menu named *Users and Permissions*. Using the menus included under this point, the administrator of the site can manage different types of permission levels. The level of access is achieved by classifying the users into different groups, whereby each group can have a different type of permission level. Here, existing groups can be used or new groups can be created. The use cases presented in this section handle the process of inviting users to the recent site classifying those users according to their responsibilities in the various departments of ShoptiExperts.

Use Case 1.1: Manage Site Owners

Each user should be classified into a group having an underlying permission level. The most widely used groups out of the box are visitors, members, and owners. The following three exercises are specific to this use case:

- **Exercise 1.1.1—Analyze "SharePoint Permission Levels"**: Navigate to the *Site Permissions* menu. By clicking the *Permission Levels* button, the accompanying page appears, on which all out of the box types of permission levels are listed. Have a look at all these and take note of the different levels.

- **Exercise 1.1.2—Utilize "SharePoint Permission Levels"**: Based on the preceding exercise, mention the members of ShoptiExperts who should be granted the accompanying level of permission.

- **Exercise 1.1.3—Grant Permission to "Owners of ShoptiExperts"**: Click the *Owners* group and list all users who are classified as part of this group. Add the user *Software Manager* to this group. At the end, two users should be classified as *Owners of ShoptiExperts*.

Use Case 1.2: Manage Users' Permissions

As noted above, different user groups exist. Until now, only the site owners have had access to SharePoint. To invite other users, other groups should be used, as in the following two exercises:

- **Exercise 1.2.1—Grant Permissions to "Readers, Designers, and Approvers"**: Navigate to the *People and Groups* menu and add the users *External Director1* and *External Director2* to the accompanying group, so that those users have permission to read information, including list items and documents. Classify users *Office Expert1* and *Office Expert2* into the accompanying group, so that they can design, which means also that they can view, add, update, delete, approve, and customize information. Finally, classify users *Strategic Director*, *Operative Manager*, and *Software Manager* as users in the accompanying group, so that they, too, can approve content, pages, items, etc.

- **Exercise 1.2.2—Grant Permissions to "Contributors"**: The permanent staff not already invited to the SharePoint site should be able to contribute to it. Navigate to the *People and Groups* menu and invite those users into the related group, so that they can view, add updates, and delete list items and documents. If no such group already exists, create a new group.

Tutorial 2: Improve Social Networking

The social network in SharePoint is named My Site. After adding a user to the SharePoint farm, a My Site site is created for the user. This My Site site combines most of the features provided by other social networks; however, My Site adds new possibilities for focusing on the professional user, instead of focusing on personal ones. From a functional perspective, the My Site site can assume two directions: the profile of the owner of the My Site site and the features of My Site. The following two tutorials relate to the editing of the profile, on the one hand, and, on the other, the use and customization of features.

Use Case 2.1: Maintain My Site Profile

My Site is available by clicking *About Me*. As with other social networking sources, the user can maintain different types of details. To experience the possibilities, perform the following five exercises:

- **Exercise 2.1.1—Maintain "Basic Information"**: After navigating to your My Site and to the *Edit page*, use the *Basic Information* tab. Use the accompanying fields to describe yourself, write a short statement, upload a portrait, and describe your main areas of work.

- **Exercise 2.1.2—Maintain "Contact Information"**: After navigating to your My Site and to the *Edit page*, use the *Contact Information* tab. Use the accompanying fields to maintain your mobile phone number, your home phone number, your location, and your representative, as outlined in Table 3-1. Note that your phone number should only be visible to you.

- **Exercise 2.1.3—Maintain "Details"**: After navigating to your My Site and to the *Edit page*, use the *Details* tab. Use the accompanying fields to maintain your last ten projects, skills, two highest degrees, and three of your personal interests.

- **Exercise 2.1.4—Maintain "Newsfeed Settings"**: After navigating to your My Site and the *Edit page*, use the *Newsfeed Settings* tab. Here, indicate which topics you want to follow. Specify that you always want to be informed of information related to it and that friends can see the people you are following.

- **Exercise 2.1.5—Save Profile and Connect**: After saving your profile settings, navigate to the link *Persons*, which will navigate you to the *Following* feature. Click the accompanying button and follow all members of your department. In addition, follow all members of the executive board, all managers, and all team leaders.

Use Case 2.2: My Site Features

In addition to the profile for each user and the capability to connect with others, My Site provides additional techniques that clearly distinguish SharePoint from other social networks. To experience those, perform the following three exercises:

- **Exercise 2.2.1—Create a "Blog"**: After having navigated to My Site, click *Blog* and *Manage Categories* Remove existing categories but create two new ones: *Data Mining*, and *Text Mining*. Return and create your first post about your experiences in agile project management. Add the related categories before publishing the post by end of day.

- **Exercise 2.2.2—Manage "Documents"**: Using the *Apps* link, navigate to the application called *Documents*. Create a new folder named *Shophouse*, which should be shared with the team leader of deparment module development and all your team members. Upload two documents named *Strategy* and *Experience*, respectively, to the folder. Share the first document with the director of the firm, so that she/he can view the file.

- **Exercise 2.2.3—Customize "Links"**: Until now, SharePoint has automatically created the links shown on your My Site. To customize the links according to your needs, add the link to any web page. Maintain the link with related text.

Tutorial 3: Customize Look and Feel

Here, SharePoint branding solutions are considered, to customize your own SharePoint environment according to the look and feel required. For example, if your company has its own corporate design, including company-specific colors, the colors of the menu in SharePoint should be identical to those of the other applications you are using. Also, your company logo should be maintained and displayed in SharePoint, instead of the default logo. In SharePoint, branding can be considered on different levels. The first is to change the logo, name, and quick configuration settings. The second level is to change colors, according to your corporate design. The third level is to change the master pages used.

Use Case 3.1: Using and Customizing Themes

The minimum customization of the look and feel of SharePoint is to change the title of your site, its description, and its logo. In addition, the user can choose from a set of predefined themes. Those types of customizations can be launched after navigating to Site Settings and using the web part named *Look and Feel*. To customize the SharePoint application, do the following three exercises:

- **Exercise 3.1.1—Change "Title, description, and logo"**: Navigate to the *Title, description, and logo* menu. Type the name of the fictitious firm. Upload any logo of your firm.

- **Exercise 3.1.2—Change "Master Page"**: Navigate to the *Master Page* menu. Open a new tab in your browser and navigate to your SharePoint site. Have a look at this site and describe the principal elements that you can see. Mainly, describe the different navigation menus available. Now, choose the other available master pages (they should be Seattle and Oslo) and describe the different navigation menus available now. Based on the preceding step, choose Oslo as the master page for all channels. In addition, specify that the master page you have defined should be used by all sites inheriting from this recent site.

- **Exercise 3.1.3—Customize "Change the Look"**: Navigate to the *Change the look* menu. Describe the main options you can see, that is, the boxes that allow you to edit your site to achieve a new look and feel. Note how many different themes exist out of the box. Choose a color, orange, and choose a sans-serif font. Move on to your site and have a look at the changes.

Use Case 3.2: Customizing Navigation and Links

The elements structuring a site can also be customized. The main element most often customized is the navigation, as it is the principal means of finding information quickly. To customize the navigation, do the following five exercises:

- **Exercise 3.2.1—Customize "Page Layouts"**: Click *Add a page.* Type *Welcome to ShoptiExperts Intranet* for your new page to be created. Move to the page and navigate to the button *Page Layouts* ➤ *Page Settings.* Specify that the page layout should be *Splash.*

- **Exercise 3.2.2—Customize "Homepage"**: Navigate to *Page Image* and upload a figure illustrating the building that your company is in. Click *Preview* and describe what happens. Now, define that this page should be the starting page.

- **Exercise 3.2.3—Publish "Homepage"**: Describe whether the site is already available or if there are any issues mentioned. Decide to *Store* the page and to *Check it in.* Finally, decide to *Publish.* the web site, so that everyone can actually see it.

- **Exercise 3.2.4—Customize "Links"**: Navigate to the top root of your site. Move to the top-level menu and decide to *Edit Links.* If not already available, add a link for the page you have created in the preceding exercise. Define the link and the name of the link, which should be *Departments.* The button to be created should be the first level of the navigation.

- **Exercise 3.2.5—Customize "Managed Navigation"**: Repeat the preceding four exercises, to create a page for each department. After that, each link will be on the same level, which is wrong, as the different departments should be displayed as child elements of the link *Departments.* To change this, first navigate to the *Navigation* menu. Describe what you can see and edit in here. Move to the *Managed Navigation Term Set* menu and navigate to *Site Navigation.* Right-click one existing term and describe the options you have. Now, move the terms, so that the department pages appear below the departments link. Finally, decide to again *Edit Links.* Change the order of the links accordingly.

Tutorial 4: Integrate Applications

Each application in SharePoint provides functional features to store and manage content according to the type of information to be administrated. Two main types of applications exist. The persons having the attendant right can create an application. On a site level, this is usually the site collection administrator. Any application can be added by using the *Add an app* button.

Use Case 4.1: Adding and Customizing Lists

Each list can be customized according to the content types to be included, the rights to manage the list, and its views, i.e., the way in which the list is presented to different types of users. To experience the functionalities, do the following five exercises:

- **Exercise 4.1.1—Understand "Custom List"**: Add a list application named *List*. Have a look at the ribbon of the list you created. List the buttons included in the *List* button, with a brief explanation.

- **Exercise 4.1.2—Create "Columns"**: After you have experienced the functionalities of a list, create one column of the type *Single line of text* with *the name Surname*. Rename the *Title* column *Name* using *List Settings. Modify View,* so that *Surname* has the first position and *Name* has the second position. Then, create an item for each of your colleagues.

- **Exercise 4.1.3—Create "Metadata Columns"**: Until now, the columns *Department, Role,* and *Representative* have been missing. The two former columns are stored as formal metadata (taxonomy). To integrate them, create two columns of the *Managed Metadata* type, with the names as given. For each of the two columns, create a new term, using *Customize your term set,* with the relationships provided in Figure 3-1, respectively. Finally, assign to each item (person) the accompanying metadata (see Table 3-1 and Table 3-2).

- **Exercise 4.1.4—Create "Person Columns 1"**: The column still missing is the *Representative* column. To resolve this, create a column of type *Person or Group*. The representative should be included in the list using the *Last name* of the other person. Finally, for all items in the list created, maintain the representative, as indicated (see Table 3-1 and Table 3-2).

- **Exercise 4.1.5—Create "Custom Views"**: Finally, create a new default view that has limited information. More precisely, this is a list named *Roles* that only lists the *Role* and *Name* of the person and her/his *Surname*. To do this, click *Create View* in the *List* tab and add a *Standard View*. Edit the position of the columns. Edit the position of the columns having *Role* as the first column and sort items by this column.

Use Case 4.2: Adding and Customizing Libraries

Libraries store different types of documents. Like lists, each library can be customized according to your needs. To experience the functionalities, do the following four exercises:

- **Exercise 4.2.1—Understand "Document Library"**: Add a *Document Library* with the same name. Have a look at the ribbon of the library you have created. Here, the tab *Library* is included, to customize the library according to your needs. List the buttons included in this tab, with a brief explanation.

- **Exercise 4.2.2—Create "Person Columns 2"**: After you have experienced the functionalities, create one column of the type *Person or Group*, with the name *Consultant*. In addition, enable *Enterprise Keywords* for this library, using *Library Settings* and *Enterprise Metadata* and *Keyword Settings*. Do not share the keywords with your My Site. Modify the view of your library, so that a new column is created to manage *Enterprise Keywords*.

- **Exercise 4.2.3—Create "Metadata Columns"**: Add the columns *Check In Comment, Created, Created By, Edit,* and *Version* to your library. Afterward, upload five Excel files.

- **Exercise 4.2.4—Create "Personal View"**: Finally, create a new view that only shows documents uploaded by you. To do so, filter in the accompanying column for your own account, using *Library Settings*. Create another view, to see the documents created by your team members.

Use Case 4.3: Adding Workflows to Applications

Integrating workflows into SharePoint allows standardization of processes. In business, work often has to be approved. In SharePoint, this is realized with Approval Workflow. Automatize the process as follows:

- **Exercise 4.3.1—Activate "Workflows"**: Navigate to the site collection features menu included in *Site Settings* and select *Site Collection Administration*." Activate the feature named *Workflows*, which allows you to access the desired workflow.

- **Exercise 4.3.2—Manage "Approval Workflow"**: Navigate to the document library implemented in the preceding use case. In *Library Settings*, decide to *Add a Workflow*. Describe which workflows are available. Decide to use the workflow named *Approval—SharePoint 2010"* and name it *Document Approval*. Define that the workflow can be started manually, that, when uploading new items, the workflow will start automatically, and that changing an item will also automatically restart the workflow. Decide that the documents administrated using this workflow should be assigned to the manager of the operations management team. Request that the document be checked and approved. Specify that any change to the workflow will result in a rejection of a document.

Tutorial 5: Using Metadata Techniques

In SharePoint, two main types of metadata techniques exist: Managed Metadata (taxonomy), and Enterprise Metadata (folksonomy). The former technique is based on formal concepts summarized inside a set of terms. The latter technique is based, in general, on informal concepts that are part of a folksonomy, and, in most systems, on what are known as tags.

Use Case 5.1: Using Managed Metadata Techniques

Imagine that you are the manager of the operations management department and that you want to create a uniform document workspace for all the members of your team. You have realized that the ordinary functionalities of folders are not sufficient, as all your members must manage various projects. Because of this, you want a document workspace that considers managed metadata (see Figure 3-2). To do this, do the following three exercises:

- **Exercise 5.1.1—Add "Managed Metadata Document Library"**: Add a new column named *Taxonomy* of type *Managed Metadata,* to your library, as created in the previous use case. Add the column to the default view.

- **Exercise 5.1.2—Customize "Term Set"**: Move to *Term Set Settings* and decide to *Customize your term set.* Implement the taxonomy illustrated in Figure 3-2 (instead of *Document Workspace,* the root concept *Taxonomy* can remain). Return to your library and explain the changes.

- **Exercise 5.1.3—Understand "Metadata Document Library"**: Add a document, *Specification* to your library. Decide to add the accompanying term *Specification Documents* as a property of the document to be uploaded. Add to your library additional documents describing change requests, documenting modules, and describing project plans. For the new documents, assert the accompanying (unique) term. Filter for different documents, using this column, and explain the experience.

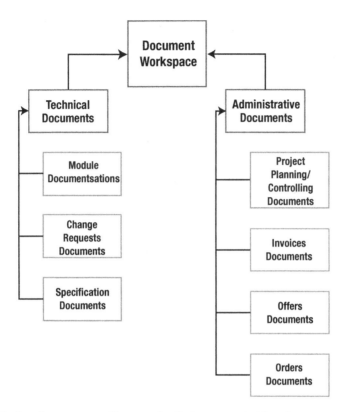

Figure 3-2. Sample taxonomy of how to classify documents inside a document workspace for various projects following a formal structure

Use Case 5.2: Using Enterprise Metadata Techniques

As it is often not sufficient to use only formal metadata, it is preferable to add informal metadata to each document. For managing projects, for example, those tags can define the name of the project or the name of the client. For integrating informal metadata, do the following three exercises:

- **Exercise 5.2.1—Allow "Enterprise Metadata":** Move to the library you created in the preceding exercise. Navigate to *Library Settings* and to the menu named *Enterprise Metadata and Keywords Settings*. Decide to add an *Enterprise Keyword* column. Edit the existing documents and assert for each document the *Client* as *Enterprise Keyword*. Note that the keywords should be in the form *Customer 1*, *Customer 2*, and *Customer 3*, and two documents should have the same customer. Filter for client-specific documents.

- **Exercise 5.2.2—Integrate "Three State Workflow"**: Add an additional column *Three State*, which should be of the type *Choice*. Define that the first choice should be *Draft*, second choice *In Revision*, and third choice *Accepted*.

- **Exercise 5.2.3—Start "Three State Workflow"**: Navigate to *Workflow Settings* and decide to *Add a workflow* of the type *Three State Workflow*, named *Document Status*. Choose that a new item added to the library will start this workflow. On the next page, leave the settings as default. Add a new document to your library and describe what happens with the *Three State* column. Describe the workflow history.

Tutorial 6: Improving Search Experience

Finding the right information at the right time is the most critical issue in information management. The techniques to find the right content are supported by metadata techniques (treated in the preceding tutorial) but also through intelligent search centers. SharePoint offers two templates to support intelligent search. A basic search center, on the one hand, and an enterprise search center, on the other, allowing more customization. Regardless of which of these two centers is used, a center can be added to a site, by adding a new subsite or creating a distinct site collection.

Use Case 6.1: Creating an Enterprise Search Center

Creating a search template based on a template is the condition for improving the search experience. To do so, and to integrate the center, do the following:

- **Exercise 6.1.1 —Add "Enterprise Search Center"**: Navigate to *Site Settings* ➤ *Site Collection Administration*, and, finally, *Site Collection Features*. Activate the feature named *SharePoint Server Publishing Infrastructure*. Navigate to *Site Contents* and decide to *Add Sub Site* of the type *Enterprise Search Center*. Give the subsite the title *Search Center*, which will have the URL .../searchcenter. Decide to use the top link bar from the parent site.

- **Exercise 6.1.2—Modify "Search URL"**: Navigate to *Site Settings* ➤ *Search* ➤ *Search Settings*. Enter the URL of your center, created in the preceding exercise, as *Search Center URL*.

- **Exercise 6.1.3—Analyze "Result Page"**: Go to your top-level site and search for *Operative Management*. You should afterward be directed to the result page showing your search query results. Describe how your search results are displayed. Edit the page using the dial, which will now highlight the already included web parts.

Use Case 6.2: Customizing a Search Center

As we have created an enterprise search center in the previous use case, the search center can be customized according to specific requirements. To customize the search center do the following two excercises:

- **Exercise 6.2.1 —Customize "Result Page"**: Navigate to the result page and edit this page. Navigate to the *Search Results* web part and decide to *Edit Web Part*. Using the settings tab, specify that *Show View Duplicates link* and *Show sort dropdown* should be active. Describe the other settings that you could modify by using this tab.

- **Exercise 6.2.2—Customize "Faceted Search"**: Navigate to the *Refinement* web part and decide to *Edit Web Part*. Decide to *Choose Refiners*. Mention all the refiners that you could add. Finally, from the "Available refiners," choose the refiners named *Languages*, *Size*, and *Tags*. Decide to newly sort the refiners and to further specify the refiners. For the refiner *Languages*, define that the maximum number of refiner values should be ten. For the refiner *Size*, define that the *Display name* should be *File size*. For the refiner *Tags*, define that the *Display template* should be of the type *Multi-value Refinement Item*. For all three refiners, mention the other settings that you could further define (not duplicated settings). Finally, make the new and customized search center for all users visible.

Tutorial 7: Managing Projects

Managing tasks is essential in projects, to ensure that particular aspects are performed on time and on budget. SharePoint provides its own project workspace, which is aimed at supporting the main functionalities required for project management. Its main element is the preconfigured application named Tasks, which is a list in SharePoint to manage tasks on different levels.

Use Case 7.1: Creating Tasks in Projects

Tasks in projects can be stored in the corresponding application. The tasks, which are list items, can have dependencies between each other, for example, if one task must be completed before another can begin. For creating tasks in projects absolve three exercises:

- **Exercise 7.1.1—Add "Project Workspace":** Navigate to *Site Contents* and decide to *Add Sub Site* of the type *Project Site*. Give the subsite the title *Project Workspace*, which will have the URL ... /projectworkspace. Decide not to use the top link bar from the parent site.

- **Exercise 7.1.2—Manage "Project Dashboard":** In the main navigation of your SharePoint site, go to *Edit Links*, so that you can add the project that you created in the preceding exercise as first-level link to your global navigation. Decide to use unique permissions for this subsite. Describe the start page of the workspace that you have created. On your start page of this subsite, click the *Working on a deadline* box and describe what happens to your start page.

- **Exercise 7.1.3—Manage "Main Project Tasks":** Edit the list named *Tasks*. Add two tasks: *Task A*, and *Task B*. Both tasks should be assigned to technicians. Through using *Show More*, specify that *Task B* is the *Predecessor* of *Task B*.

Use Case 7.2: Managing Tasks in Projects

Often, tasks in projects consist of other tasks performing as subtasks of a bigger task. This can also be managed inside SharePoint. In addition, each subtask can also be assigned to other SharePoint users. For managing tasks in projects absolve two exercises:

- **Exercise 7.2.1—Manage "Sub Tasks":** For each task, subtasks should be created. For *Task A*, create the subtasks *Task A.1*, *Task A.2*, and *Task A.3*. For *Task B*, the subtasks *Task B.1*, *Task B.2*, and *Task B.3* should be created. All subtasks of *Task A* should be assigned to the leader of the team being responsible for developing modules. All the subtasks of *Task B* should be assigned to the leader of the team being responsible for design and support.

- **Exercise 7.2.2—Manage "Project Timeline"**: For all tasks and subtasks, specify any start and due date. For each task, decide that it should be added to the time line (*Add to Timeline*). Navigate to the timeline menu and decide that the time line should be *Display as Callout*. Describe the changes.

Conclusion

This chapter presented hands-on tutorials to practically experience the capabilities of Microsoft SharePoint Server 2016. In total, seven different tutorials including various use cases were presented, all based on real-world scenarios. Before starting with the tutorials, the methodology informing the tutorials was presented. A fictitious firm was presented, for which hands-on use cases were built. In addition, preparations required to perform the use cases were also given. Afterward, the tutorials were discussed, including various use cases concerning user management, for improving social networking, customizing the look and feel of SharePoint, integrating applications, using metadata techniques, improving search experience, and managing tasks in projects.

Best Practice Scenarios

The functionalities of SharePoint are extensive, as it is a leading enterprise content management system and, as such, handles different aspects of content management within one application. Because the functionalities of SharePoint are extensive and are supplemented by a huge number of users with different knowledge and familiarity who use the application more or less frequently, it is absolutely necessary to define how the application should be used in general and to define how the underlying workplaces are differentiated from one another. Both aspects avoid uncontrolled and unregulated use of the application, which would, of course, lead to negative aspects, such as user dissatisfaction and uncontrolled growth. To avoid these, rules governing how to manage and administrate the application must be set up before use. In addition, a mechanism that constantly and frequently scrutinizes the initial setup rules and adjusts those, according to the feedback of the users or in cases of anomalies, must be supported. However, understanding which issues should be part of such rules, and how the mechanism to achieve and implement adjustments must be made manifest, is not straightforward, because of two principal barriers.

The first barrier exists because it is crucial to understanding the purpose and elements of such rules and mechanisms in detail. Often, rules are set up that do not cover all aspects: existing rules overlap or the mechanism to constantly scrutinize them disappears after a while. The second barrier exists because the aim of the SharePoint templates, including the underlying technologies, must be interpreted correctly with regard to the use cases to be considered.

© Heiko Angermann 2017
H. Angermann, *Manager's Guide to SharePoint Server 2016*,
https://doi.org/10.1007/978-1-4842-3045-9_4

Often, users employ the provided functionalities in an impetuous manner. This is because they do not consider the global impacts of using a specific technique but focus instead on the quickest solution at a particular moment. This chapter is presented to help users scale both barriers and to ultimately avoid user dissatisfaction, uncontrolled growth of an application, and the wrong utilization of SharePoint techniques. The solution to the first barrier is covered by explaining best practices with regard to the methodology of a so-called governance model. Such a model defines the rules to be set up and gives advice about control and adjustment of the rules. Giving best practices regarding the use of the different types of SharePoint templates lifts the second barrier. How the most widely used templates are utilized to support the different use cases is discussed in detail, to that end. In addition to an explanation of how to control the usage and differentiate between particular techniques, various additional tools allowing for improved manageability of the web application, customization of the web application, standardization and automation, usability and integration of data being provided outside SharePoint, and structuring a huge amount of data using metadata techniques are explained in this chapter.

The remainder of this chapter is organized as follows. The first section begins by discussing various governance best practice models. These include an explanation of how to set up a governance committee and, of course, the associated governance plan. Afterward, best practices regarding the final use of the different types of site collection and site templates are given in the second section. In the third section, tools to more effectively manage a SharePoint web application are discussed, including the underlying SharePoint site-collections, sites, and pages. This includes a discussion about tools provided directly by Microsoft to manage and customize the SharePoint web application. In addition, tools presented by third party solution providers, which extensively expand the SharePoint out of the box functionalities regarding the most important aspects, are presented. These regard the integration and usage of more complex workflows, the effective connection of SharePoint with external data sources, as well as a more effective use and integration of metadata techniques. The chapter concludes with this section.

Best Practices Governance Model

A governance model refers to roles and processes inside an enterprise that serve as a guideline for fulfilling, sustaining, and extending the IT planning.[1] Such a model is important to define and control how users of your SharePoint environment will employ the site(s). The benefits, in detail, as well as the elements of the model are explained in this section.

---

[1] Techopedia, "Governance Plan," www.techopedia.com/definition/2910/governance-plan, accessed May 30, 2017.

Benefits of a Governance Model

Setting up a governance model before starting to use the application, and through constantly adjusting the rules, will mainly avoid uncontrolled growth of the application and support its correct use. The four main improvements are as follows[2]:

- **Organizing content** will improve the application, as it lets the site user know when a new subsite should be created, instead of creating another list or library to store information on a site already storing a large amount of heterogeneous data.

- **Storage reduction** will be improved, as a governance model includes rules for semiautomatically removing unnecessary content and subsites. This reduces costs and provides a controlled amount of storage space, which, in turn, limits obsolete content from being resulted for search queries.

- **Access management** will be improved, as the model includes rules ensuring that those having access to a page, subsite, etc. Are actually the people who should have access to it, and that they can only perform allowed operations.

- **Template usage** will strongly be improved, as the model ensures that owners of a subsite or site collection are able to use the templates only as required, instead of allowing site owners to use any template for single use case.

Elements of a Governance Model

Each model consists of two elements: a **governance committee** and a **governance plan**. The committee is a group of users responsible for defining, setting up, and constantly improving the model. The governance plan is the collection of the rules ultimately defining the governance model.

---

[2]Microsoft, "Overview: Best Practices for Managing How People Use Your Team Site," https://support.office.com/en-us/article/Overview-best-practices-for-managing-how-people-use-your-team-site-95e83c3d-e1b0-4aae-9d08-e94dcaa4942e, accessed May 30, 2017.

Establishing a Governance Committee

For developing a governance plan, a governance committee should be appointed.[3] This committee should be a group of SharePoint users with different knowledge of the system, having varying familiarity with the system, and having different levels of access to the system. It is not recommended to have only SharePoint experts on this committee, as different types of feedback are required to constantly improve the SharePoint web application.

The aim and responsibility of the committee are to set up the governance policies (i.e., the rules) to discuss the SharePoint issues and anomalies, to collect users' feedback, and to constantly and frequently update the governance plan. Even if there are no problems with the site, users' feedback must be reviewed constantly. By holding regular meetings, each plan becomes not merely a written document. Moreover, a governance plan is an ongoing process that must be perpetually improved. Logically, it is also very important to forward any changes in the governance plan to users and to train users according to the new rules and processes.

Establishing a Governance Plan

The amount of governance usually depends on the type of site.[4] Personal sites, e.g., My Sites, require the lowest amount of governance, illustrated in Figure 4-1. Sites for administrating projects or workspaces, in general, require the second least amount of governance, as usually not as many users have access to a single workspace. Sites being provided to groups or teams require more governance, as the number of users having access to these types of sites is usually greater. Logically, sites to which a whole department has access require more governance, as do other team sites. Finally, the top-level site of the SharePoint environment requires the most amount of governance, as all users have access to this site. The issues of most concern to a governance committee can be divided into 12 main areas, as follows[5]:

---

[3]Gregory Zelfond, "How to Implement SharePoint Governance," SharePoint Maven, http://sharepointmaven.com/implement-sharepoint-governance/, November 21, 2016.
[4]Microsoft, "What Is Governance in SharePoint 2013?," https://technet.microsoft.com/en-us/library/cc263356.aspx, accessed May 30, 2017.
[5]Microsoft, " Overview: Best Practices for Managing How People Use Your Team Site," https://support.office.com/en-us/article/Overview-best-practices-for-managing-how-people-use-your-team-site-95e83c3d-e1b0-4aae-9d08-e94dcaa4942e, accessed May 30, 2017.

- **Information architecture** considers how the information and content are organized and ultimately shown to users. Having a hierarchical structure of the web application achieves this. Such a structure considers the included site-collections, the subsites, as well as the included pages and applications. The main topics are what kind of content will be managed on the different site levels, how the information will be presented, how the different levels are considered in the navigation, how specific audiences will be targeted, and how users will be able to find the content stored on different levels.

- **Storage limits** are important if the amount of storage is limited. If so, it must be ensured that no obsolete or redundant information is stored in SharePoint. In addition, criteria must be defined that clarify when content is outdated and, based on that, how the outdated content must be removed or archived semiautomatically.

- **Site creation** considers strategies to be adopted by users in creating subsites. The main considerations are who should be allowed to create subsites, if the subsites must be approved before their creation, which templates should be allowed, how much information can be stored, and when should the site be deleted.

- **Site life cycle and retirement** are considerations that are required in any review of existing sites. These are important, as, often, sites are not used permanently, for example, a project site of a completed project. Logically, this site should be removed.

- **Permission management** considers the roles and types of access users can be granted to a site. In general, the level of permission a user is granted should be the lowest level required to perform his or her assigned tasks. It is also recommended that people be added to standard groups having the already existing permission levels. For managing the access to different levels of sites, the permission levels and the assignment of users to specific groups can be inherited.

- **Classification of information** is required to help people find the desired data and information. In SharePoint, two types of metadata techniques exist to classify information. **Managed Metadata** lets users classify the information via taxonomy. **Enterprise Keywords** lets users classify the information being stored via folksonomy. Mixing both techniques is the best practice for quickly finding the desired information promptly.

- **Data protection** is necessary to protect data from accidental loss. To overcome accidental loss, back up data regularly and store the backups according to different rules and systems.

- **Navigation** is a necessary consideration, as it is, after the search center, the main element to help users find the information and data they desire. The navigations to be included should be precise but not too extensive. **Global navigation** should not extend beyond three levels. **Local navigation** should be a maximum of two levels, preferably only one level, to quickly find the information required for this fine-granular place.

- **Search** must also be considered, as it is the core element in the search for information. Having large amounts of information on the web application requires that search results be filtered. The filtering must be performed automatically, by showing only the results of a specific site or, manually, by providing advanced filtering techniques (e.g., faceted search).

- **Customization** is a required consideration, as each enterprise usually has its own corporate design. This design provides a consistent look and feel over all channels used by the firm (e.g., intranet and internet).

- **Roles and responsibilities** must ensure that the site is performing consistently and that all users know what they are doing. This involves the issues of setting up a team capable of supporting and training users, for example, by having a designated application manager.

- **Automatization** is an important consideration, as many tasks are performed automatically by the system itself. The main issues here are to consider the workflows required for automatizing and standardizing tasks.

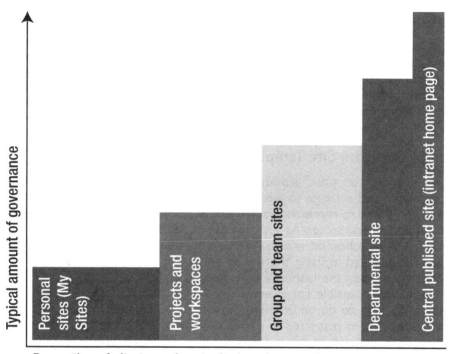

Figure 4-1. The increasing volume of governance required depends on the complexity and diversity of the Sharepoint web application required[6]

Best Practices Template Usage

In SharePoint, various templates exist to create site-collections and sites. The three different types of site collection and site templates can be considered as preconfigured workplaces that include applications and settings to satisfy a specific business task. The collaboration templates aim to improve collaboration when different persons work on a project, want to share knowledge, or work together as a team. The enterprise templates manage sensitive information, for example, documents and records, or administrate the search process. Publishing templates, in contrast, are aimed at publishing content destined for the web, instead of known users. To better help readers decide which template to use for a specific goal, the most important templates are discussed in detail following.

[6]Microsoft, "What Is Governance in SharePoint 2013?" https://technet.microsoft.com/en-us/library/cc263356.aspx, accessed May 30, 2017.

Using Collaboration Templates

Collaboration templates improve collaboration between staff working in any kind of constellation. The most widely used templates in this category are the team site template and the project site template. Other templates are the blog template, the developer site template, and the community site template, which, in contrast to the other two templates, are more rarely used.

Using the Team Site Template

The Team Site template provides a preconfigured place, including relevant applications and settings, to work together as group users. In practice, this template is used to represent a static unit of a firm, e.g., a team, a department, or a more general sector. As such, the use of this template highly depends on the type of team, how many of its members are using this site, and the flexibility users are allowed in using the site. In general, it is recommended that the content stored on the team site be organized, and the access by single users be as limited as possible. For example, users should be allowed only to do what they really have to do, and the customization and creation of new lists and libraries should be restricted to a small number of users, e.g., site owners and designers. In addition, as this is one of the more complex templates, a training plan should be established to show each user how to use the team site and what the purpose of this type of site is. In summary, the following suggestions should be considered and should be part of the overall governance model[7]:

- **Permission levels** to be used on the site should be established. As permissions levels, the levels of the parent site can be used, or unique permission levels can be created.

- **Consistency and intuitiveness** must be considered. These are mainly achieved through a clear differentiation between the applications and pages used and by not having multiple places to administrate similar types of information.

- **Functional navigation** allows quick browsing through the site and will highly support users in finding the right information at the right time. Therefore, it is very important to distinguish between the types of SharePoint navigations (local and global) and decide on the underlying technique (managed or custom).

---

[7]Jon Hood, "How to Organize Your SharePoint Team Site for Optimal Results," KnowledgeWave, www.knowledgewave.com/blog/sharepoint-team-site-organization, November 10, 2015, accessed May 31, 2017.

- **Metadata** will strongly support structuring the content and data to be managed. In practice, it is highly recommended that both metadata techniques, folksonomy and taxonomy, be used in tandem. Therefore, it is crucial to avoid ambiguity between folksonomical tags and to have a semantically rich taxonomy. It is best practice to use both techniques in common.

Using the Project Site Template

The Project Site template provides a preconfigured location, including relevant applications and settings, from which to work with other users on a project. In practice, this template is used in the workplace, to share project-related documents, to see the status of a project, and to manage the tasks related to the project. In contrast to the template for managing a team, this type of site should be used for dynamic constellations, rather than for permanent teams. It is highly recommended to use this site only for active projects and to have a separate project site for each project. This will avoid mixing tasks of different projects, mixing documents required for different projects, and, of course, losing control over an active project. The template provided by SharePoint is mainly focused on administrative tasks, managing documents, and determining the project status, not to replace issue-tracking systems. For managing projects in SharePoint with the Project Site template, the following suggestions are offered[8]:

- **Informative start page** is important, as it performs as a dashboard, giving members a summary of work, goals, project status, as well as highlighting upcoming events. The start page should summarize only the most important details and events. It should not show details relevant only to specific members.

- **Project planning** is crucial to effectively manage the project. In SharePoint, global navigation can be used for planning a project. The navigation can include a list of brief status updates to inform stakeholders, a document library storing project documents, and a task list to schedule the project in detail.

---

[8]Billy Guinan, "Using SharePoint for Project Management—An Overview," BrightWork, www.brightwork.com/blog/using-sharepoint-2013-project-management-overview, January 27, 2017.

- **Task tracking** is important for meeting deadlines. To do so, it is most important that each member knows exactly what his/her tasks are and their status. In SharePoint, this can be achieved by having different views for the task list, for example, one global view for the project manager and separate views for each team member, showing only the tasks that are assigned to the user.

- **Visualization and reporting** are necessary to quickly communicate the status of a project. In SharePoint, this can be achieved by setting up project status reports, including key performance indicators (KPIs) with red, amber, green indicators, and by including comment columns.

Using Enterprise Templates

Enterprise templates aim to help manage sensitive content and information. The most widely used templates of this category are the document center template and the enterprise search center template. Other templates in this category are: in-place hold policy center, ediscovery center, records center, compliance policy center, my site host, and community portal, in addition to the basic enterprise search center template.

Using the Document Center Template

The Document Center template offers a site to manage documents at the enterprise level, via a document management system. Therefore, it is important to distinguish between this and the document library application, which is also used to store and administrate documents. In contrast to the library, the document center site and site collection template is a global place to store documents, instead of an application that is used by single sites. As such, it allows users to focus only on documents and collaborate on documents in a single place. This is important, as depending on the size and purpose of the enterprise, many different documents may exist that concern multiple teams. For managing documents, the establishment of document taxonomy is inevitable. This taxonomy should consider all possible types of documents, so that each document is assigned the right formal concept. In addition, folksonomical keywords can be used to distinguish even better between the documents sharing a single taxonomical concept, or to more quickly filter for documents. For managing documents inside a document center, the following five suggestions should be considered[9]:

---

[9]Gregory Zelfond, "The Top 5 Best Practices for Document Management in SharePoint," SharePoint Maven, http://sharepointmaven.com/top-5-best-practices-document-management-sharepoint/, January 15, 2014.

- **Metadata usage** is the most crucial element when storing documents. Structuring documents in folders, as provided by file systems, has to be strictly avoided, as those do not support quickly finding the desired documents. For using metadata to administrate documents, it is recommended to have a mix of taxonomy and folksonomy.

- **Content types** can be used for automatically assigning documents with the right metadata information. For example, if a document entitled "Meeting Minutes" is uploaded in a PowerPoint file format, SharePoint can automatically recognize the underlying content type and assign the related keywords.

- **Alert usage** is helpful to avoid abuse of the site and misleading operations. The owner of the site should always be automatically informed about what is happening on the site. In SharePoint, this can be achieved by setting up alerts, always informing the relevant users of what is happening.

- **Versioning control** ensures restoration of previous versions of a document and allows users to check which changes have been made across versions. Therefore, it is necessary to use SharePoint's Check-In/-Out feature to prevent accidental modification of the same version by multiple users at the same time.

- **Creating views** can support faster finding of desired information. Therefore, different views based on the underlying metadata are recommended. In addition, views for different purposes or persons/teams should be created, allowing for quicker browsing through document libraries.

Using the Enterprise Search Center Template

The Enterprise Search Center template helps users to find the content and information they require more quickly. A search center in SharePoint is similar to other well-known search engine machines. Like those, a SharePoint search center provides a starting page that includes a search slot to perform search queries. After querying for a term or phrase, an overview of search results appears, listing all results satisfying the query. From a user's perspective, the most important steps when implementing a SharePoint search center are the establishment of faceted search techniques. In SharePoint, this is achieved by setting up what are known as search verticals and refiners. The former technique is displayed under the search slot. By default, there are four verticals:

everything, people, conversations, and videos. Through these, the user can limit the displayed search results, by filtering for the relevant type of content, except if the user is filtering for everything. The last-mentioned technique is shown in addition to the search results. Default refiners are, for example, result type, author, modified date, and size. By using these refiners, a user can additionally filter for the desired documents. Both types of faceted search can be configured in SharePoint, depending on the purpose of the search center. For improving the search experience, the following should be considered:

- **Search center integration** means that the search can be performed directly on the site, instead of by performing search queries isolated in the search center.

- **Metadata usage** is another crucial aspect to improve this type of site. If the data is organized in a structured manner, and the information is consistently assigned with the correct metadata, the search experience will be greatly improved. The reason is that the underlying crawler uses this metadata information to index the possible query results.

- **Using refiners** will additionally improve the search experience. In SharePoint, a large number of predefined refiners exist, which just have to be added to the search center. Additionally, personal refiners can be created to customize the search experience.

- **Crawling schedules** has two benefits: (1) larger distances between the schedules, which save resources but have the drawback of not always giving the latest status of the query results; and (2) smaller distances, which, in contrast, require hardware resources but ensure that the latest status for the query results is always provided. In practice, to crawl and index the documents every day, e.g., every night, is recommended.

Using Publishing Site Templates

Publishing templates provide an environment in which to publish information on the web as an internet, intranet, or extranet presence. Again, two templates are most widely used. The most popular site collection template is pubishing portal, which is known as publishing site, if the template is used on a site level. Other templates are the product catalog template, to administrate product-related content, and the enterprise wiki template, to provide a place for managing intellectual property.

The publishing site template is geared toward publishing content on the web. As such, two templates exist. The first template is the **Publishing Site** template. The second template is **Publishing Site with workflow**. Both templates are similar. The only difference is that the latter template includes a workflow for approving the pages to be published. In practice, not many internet sites are realized using SharePoint. The reason is that SharePoint is an enterprise content management system (ECMS), and publishing web sites are only a single aspect of ECMS. Other systems, in contrast, focus only on publishing sites for the Web—web content management system (WCMS). Setting up an Internet site with WCMS is, in practice, much faster than with SharePoint, as they are less complex. In addition, recent WCMS provide much better branding technologies. Thus, SharePoint's publishing template is mainly used by publishing sites as an intranet, or by enterprises that do not want to use another system for publishing on the web, and through this avoid redundant content. The following issues must be considered before setting up a SharePoint publishing site:

- **Intuitive navigation** allows visitors to browse through the site quickly and will strongly support finding the desired information. Therefore, it is most important to have a semantically rich navigation that is not too big. In addition, it is good practice to have only a single navigation on internet sites. In SharePoint, the used **Master Page** can consider this.

- **Approval process** is necessary to ensure that the right information is published and that this information does not include any errors. In SharePoint, this can be achieved by using the related workflows, i.e., **Approval Workflow**.

- **SharePoint branding** is required to have the site take into account the corporate design of a firm. In SharePoint, branding can be performed on different levels. First, another **Composed Look** can be chosen. Second, using specific color **Themes** can customize the composed look. Third, the underlying **Master Page** can be customized.

- **Web parts** are needed to make the site dynamic. Web parts in SharePoint allow the querying and, ultimately, displaying of content stored on other pages. In addition, the web parts can be configured to always query for the latest content, for the most relevant content, or content published by specific persons.

Best Practices Additional Tools

Different tools exist to more effectively manage SharePoint web applications. These deal with the integration of more complex workflows, instead those provided out of the box, allow a more effective connection of SharePoint with external data sources, instead of those provided out of the box, as well as techniques to more effectively deal with the administration of metadata. For all three purposes, the additional tools are either provided by Microsoft itself or by third party solution providers. The following section presents the most popular and useful tools.

Microsoft Products

To better manage SharePoint web applications, and to customize the SharePoint site, Microsoft provides its own tools. The most important tool is the Microsoft SharePoint Designer, which helps to more effectively manage the SharePoint web applications, instead of using the browser. Another important tool is Microsoft SharePoint Color Palette Tool. This tool is designed for branding the SharePoint web application according to a corporate design (corporate identity across different channels and applications). Both tools are available open source.

Managing SharePoint with SharePoint Designer

As noted, SharePoint Designer is a tool to manage SharePoint web applications more efficiently, ensuring better structure and, by this, less time-consumption, rather than the browser, desktop application shown in Figure 4-2. The tool allows for modification of the application from a functional perspective, such as creating, importing, and editing page layouts, templates, styles, sites, pages, applications, data sources, and workflows. Therefore, this software strongly supports building and customizing the SharePoint sites, not only the design of SharePoint, as the name might misleadingly imply. No fee must be paid to download and use this very helpful editor.[10]

---

[10]Microsoft, "SharePoint Designer 2013," Microsoft Download Center, www.microsoft.com/en-us/download/details.aspx?id=35491, accessed May 30, 2017.

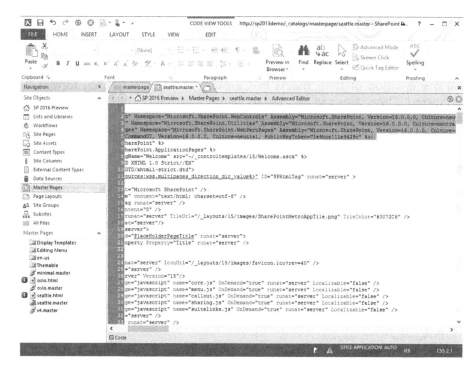

Figure 4-2. A sample user interface of the Microsoft SharePoint Designer local desktop application 2013, showing the editing of source code[11]

All operations performed on the SharePoint site itself can also be performed with SharePoint Designer. Advanced SharePoint users, usually the owners of the SharePoint site, avail themselves of this software to more quickly customize the site, including pages, lists, and libraries, instead of always clicking through the sites on the browser. The most important tasks that can be performed using this tool are the following: creating and customizing lists and libraries, managing and creating new workflows, managing site pages and assets, administrating and customizing content types, creating and modifying site columns, managing external content types and data sources, editing and creating master pages and page layouts, managing site groups, and, finally, administrating and creating subsites.

[11]Eric Overfield, "SharePoint 2016 Preview Released—A First Look at Branding," Eric Overfield, http://ericoverfield.com/sharepoint-2016-preview-released-a-first-look-at-branding/, accessed September 24, 2017.

The editor plays also a crucial role in branding the SharePoint site. It includes an Hypertext Markup Language (HTML) editor, in which **Master Pages** and **Page Layouts** can be directly edited like other editors, e.g., Microsoft Expression Web. In addition, **Color Themes** can be directly imported, and the creation of style sheets in Cascading Style Sheet (CSS) format is supported. Those files can be used to further customize the look and feel of the site or to overwrite elements of the theme.

Branding SharePoint with Color Palette Tool

SharePoint Color Palette Tool is very helpful for branding the SharePoint site according to a corporate design. The desktop application is shown in Figure 4-3. no fee has to be paid for downloading and using the application.[12]

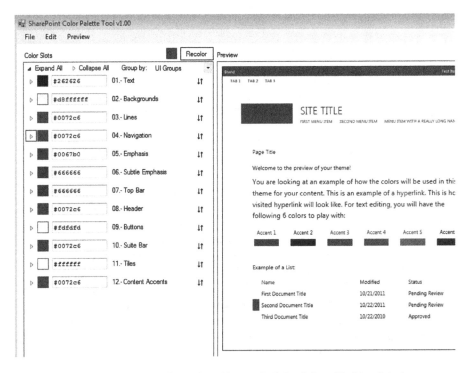

Figure 4-3. A sample user interface of the Microsoft Color Palette Tool local desktop application showing the editing of main color slots

---

[12]Microsoft,"SharePoint Color Palette Tool," Microsoft Download Center, www.microsoft. com/en-us/download/details.aspx?id=38182, accessed May 30, 2017.

With the SharePoint Color Palette Tool, the existing themes can be edited, and new color themes can be created. The tool lists as div containers all elements of the page and all color attributes that are included on a SharePoint site, e.g., the color of the text boxes (title, body, etc.), background colors (header, hover, selection, etc.), the color of lines to be used (strong lines, dialog borders, etc.), the color of the navigation (accent, hover, pressed, etc.), the color of the tab bar, color of buttons, and so on. Single color values can be defined as a hex value or can be chosen with a color picker, which automatically specifies the hex value of the color to be picked. The tool contains a WYSIWYG (what you see is what you get) editor, so that the changes are directly visible in the tool. After exporting the modified or created color theme, and uploading the file into the accompanying SharePoint list named **Theme Gallery**, those can be chosen to **Change the Look** of the SharePoint site.

Third Party Tools

Third party tools extend the functionalities provided by SharePoint out of the box, or to improve the provided services. Two critical aspects when using an ECMS are the integration of workflows and connection to the ECMS with external data sources. One other aspect is to effectively manage metadata. For this reason, most widely used third party tools are reviewed in the following sections.

Integrating Complex Workflows with Nintex

The workflows available in SharePoint out of the box have the drawback that all are sequential workflows. This means that they are aimed at very general workflow scenarios not having loops, are not designed for very large workflow operations, and are mainly based on standard processes. To allow customization of workflows, including out of the box workflows, four possibilities are considered by Microsoft:

- Out of the box workflows can be customized in the **Browser**. However, here, only nontechnical properties can be customized, e.g., the name of the workflow to be associated, etc.

- Out of the box workflows can also be customized with **SharePoint Designer**. Here, the logic, or included forms, of the workflows can be modified. Additionally, using the designer, new tasks can be included for existing workflows, or completely new sequential workflows can be created.

- Personal activities can also be added to workflows, by using **Microsoft Visual Studio**. These activities must now be provided as custom code, in order to be included. Additionally, non-declarative workflows can be created using this development application, to provide the workflows as a SharePoint solution.

- As an alternative to using a development platform, workflows can also be created by using a graphical tool, i.e., **Microsoft Visio**. The workflows to be created within this application can be imported into SharePoint Designer or Visual Studio, for further development.

The drawback of the Microsoft technologies is that the workflows are either only sequential workflows or must be developed. The latter is a very expensive undertaking, as it must be performed by a software developer and is, of course, very time-consuming. To allow more complex workflows in SharePoint without the need to develop them is to refer to other workflow management tools supporting SharePoint. The most important third party provider for SharePoint workflows is Nintex. This firm, based in Melbourne, NSW Australia, specializes in expanding Microsoft SharePoint products. Nintex has had the vision to increase productivity and efficiency of enterprises by making techniques easier to understand and to customize and implement.[13] The Nintex workflow engine has a graphical editor with the aim of functionally extending the workflow engine already provided out of the box by SharePoint. Through this, it provides a direct integration into SharePoint and its workflow foundation. In contrast to the above-mentioned possibilities provided by Microsoft, Nintex facilitates the creation of extensive state-machine workflows without any line of coding, as each workflow can be defined graphically. It provides many templates, and the predefined steps can be added simply via drag and drop.

Connecting SharePoint with Layer 2 BDLC

SharePoint provides Business Connectivity Services (BCS) out of the box. With BCS, external data resources can be integrated in SharePoint lists. For integration of external data resources, the external resource must be verified.

BCS requires a good technical understanding, and the handling required to perform these operations with SharePoint Designer must be learned. A much quicker solution for integrating almost any type of external data is to use the

---

[13]Brooke Campbell, "How to Choose the Best SharePoint Workflow Tool—OOTB vs. Nintex vs. K2," Collab365 Community, https://collab365.community/choose-best-sharepoint-workflow-tool-ootb-vs-nintext-vs-k2/, accessed January 12, 2017.

Business Data List Connector (BDLC) provided by Layer2.[14] The BDLC allows different database interfaces, e.g. Open Database Connectivity (ODBC), connection strings, as well as an editor to include SQL queries. The core benefit of using BDLC instead of BCS is the possibility to modify content types, more precisely, its columns, as well as the possibility of integrating workflows and the opportunity to update lists.

Managing Term Sets with Taxonomy Manager

SharePoint provides out of the box the **Term Store Management Tool**, to maintain taxonomies (term sets). It allows the basic functionalities, such as creating new term sets, modifying single terms, or extending existing sets.

For dealing with taxonomies to be used in SharePoint more efficiently, Layer2 provides a Taxonomy Manager.[15] This allows advanced export and import functionalities and supports the most widely used format, Simple Knowledge Organization System (SKOS), instead of only allowing taxonomies expressed in Comma Separated Value (CSV) file format. In addition, it allows management of additional SharePoint attributes, such as content classification rules, and allows updating of existing SharePoint term sets without losing classified information.

Conclusion

This chapter presented valuable best practice scenarios for Microsoft SharePoint. First, advice to be considered before implementing SharePoint inside an enterprise was given, but also suggestions on what to consider when SharePoint is already functioning. The improvements discussed were mainly achieved by explaining how a governance model should be established, including the foundation of a governance committee, and the concrete ways of setting up a comprehensive governance plan. Next, best practices regarding the use of different templates were given. Here, the most widely used collaboration, enterprise, and publishing site templates were discussed. At the end of this chapter, additional tools were identified and discussed. Such tools can help to more effectively brand, customize, and utilize SharePoint applications. These included different products provided by Microsoft, as well as various products provided by third party providers.

---

[14]Hamburg Layer 2 GmbH, "SharePoint Data Integration: Layer2 Business Data List Connector," www.layer2solutions.com/en/products/Pages/SharePoint-Business-Data-List-Connector.aspx, accessed May 30, 2017.
[15]Hamburg Layer 2 GmbH, "Layer2 Taxonomy Manager for SharePoint—Overview," www.layer2solutions.com/en/products/Pages/Taxonomy-Manager-SharePoint-2010.aspx, accessed May 30, 2017.

Hands-On Solutions

To experience the core capabilities of the SharePoint 2016 enterprise content management system practically, seven tutorials were presented in the third chapter. Specifically, tutorials were included to offer readers hands-on experience with SharePoint's different functionalities for the following: managing users' different levels of access to the web application; improving social networking in firms by creating social profiles and by using social features; more or less complicated customizing of the look and feel of the application being shown to users; integrating different types of applications, including customizing those for effective management using workflows; utilizing different types of metadata techniques to help find and structure heterogeneous information (content, documents, data); and, finally, managing and administering different types of tasks occurring in projects and teams. With the help of the tutorials, readers gained practical experience of which areas are most important for managing enterprises' content and how those areas can be covered using Microsoft SharePoint Server 2016. To help readers better translate them into a real-world environment, the tutorials were based on a fictitious firm, albeit with very real-world features.

In this chapter, solutions to the tutorials in chapter 3 are discussed in detail. Different use cases for each tutorial presented in chapter 3 are considered, including a number of exercises. This has been done to differentiate methodologically between the different existing core techniques. The solutions are presented using the same convention of not obscuring the overview and to quickly find the answers required. Because of this, each solution again includes

© Heiko Angermann 2017
H. Angermann, *Manager's Guide to SharePoint Server 2016*,
https://doi.org/10.1007/978-1-4842-3045-9_5

several use cases. In turn, each use case includes several exercises. Logically, the solutions to the tutorials and the exercises increase in complexity. However, different from the tutorials in chapter 3, each exercise is presented in detail, regardless of its complexity. By having performed the tutorials in chapter 3, this chapter can be used as a learning control or answer key, if the reader has not performed all the exercises. After doing the tutorials, and by using this chapter, readers will understand SharePoint's main capabilities, regardless of their expertise.

The remainder of this chapter is organized as follows. The first section starts by detailing how the solutions are presented. In the second section, solutions to the seven tutorials are presented. Of course, these include solutions for the use cases and exercises included in each tutorial.

Solutions Methodology and Preparation

The solutions presented aim to help understand the main technologies of SharePoint, based on those presented in chapter 3. This means that for the tutorials, which include different use cases, a step-by-step explanation is given, including how to perform and operate various techniques. In total, solutions are presented for seven areas of SharePoint 2016, covering most of the most important areas and tasks supported and covered by SharePoint: user management, improving social networking, customization of the look and feel, integration of applications, using metadata techniques, improving search experience, and managing tasks.

All the tutorials presented in chapter 3 are based on a fictional firm named ShoptiExperts. The main objective of ShoptiExperts is to implement and optimize e-commerce solutions in a B2B (business-to-business) context.[1] The focus of ShoptiExperts is on front-end design and the Shophouse modules used by the e-commerce system. Because ShoptiExperts wants to improve its internal processes, the company decided to use SharePoint. All the tutorials and, likewise, all the solutions, are based on real-world requirements to improve companies' efficiency in or by the seven areas and tasks previously mentioned. In this section, the general characteristics of the firm are outlined. These include the expectations the company has of its systems and the preparations required to implement them.

Solutions Methodology (Fictional Firm)

ShoptiExperts has 22 staff members. The different staff is organized according to different roles. Of course, the staff also is organized hierarchically in formal departments. For more details about the firm, including departments and staff, see chapter 3.

---

[1]Fictivious e-commerce system.

Before having implemented SharePoint 2016, ShoptiExperts had only used a web content management system (WCMS) to handle its online presence. In contrast to SharePoint, the WCMS focused only on one specific requirement, namely, establishing an online presence. Other information and data that the enterprise generated was spread over different file directories, electronic mail, or as printed documents. Because of this, before having implemented SharePoint, staff had problems finding the information they desired, information got lost, and, often, the information was imparted only to individual employees rather than system-wide. Those are the reasons why the firm decided to invest in Microsoft SharePoint Server 2016. After SharePoint was finally implemented, the first internal projects were to customize and use the system to get the most out of its application. These initial steps, meaning the adaptation of the application in accordance with ShoptiExperts's requirements, were performed through the tutorials.

Solutions Preparation

For understanding the solutions presented in the next section, no technical preparation is required. The solutions can also be understood without having access to a SharePoint environment, as the most important steps are also illustrated as screenshots. However, it is highly recommended that the reader complete the tutorials as preparation to understand the solutions.

Hands-On Solutions and Their Use Cases

This section allows readers to experience the solutions to the different tutorials firsthand. The solutions for the different areas of SharePoint 2016 are presented using the same convention as the tutorials themselves.

For each of the tutorials, a solution bearing the same name is presented. Again, each solution is divided into different use cases. The use cases have the same name as the tutorials presented in chapter 3. Use cases belonging to a related solution cover the same area of SharePoint. However, those differ according to the techniques used. For most solutions, the use cases build upon the use case(s) belonging to an identical resolution. As such, the use cases can be considered as phases required to achieve a functionality required in a real-world context. In addition, by dividing the tutorials into separate use cases, they can be performed independent of one another. Of course, the steps ultimately explained are presented through the exercises. Again, the same titles are used. The exercises allow the reader to understand which steps are required to fulfill a use case, that is, the steps that are necessary to satisfy a real-world and concrete requirement with SharePoint. The individual exercises and the discussion of each step required to perform these are discussed in a comprehensive manner. It follows, then, that the explanations are based on the same methodologies as for the tutorials, meaning that they reference the fictional firm and that the user assumes the role of site owner. In the end, the reader can switch between chapters (3 and 5), without losing sight of the overview and without ignoring steps that must be performed with SharePoint. In addition to the steps being explained in detail, illustrations are also provided. This graphical representation illustrates the core results that occur during the fulfillment of a use case. For this, the front end of SharePoint is shown.

■ **Note** For all solutions presented in the following section, the reader is assumed to be the employee named Operations Manager, with full access to the site. The author, Heiko Angermann, implements the solutions as Operations Manager. Because of this, the screenshots often refer to *Heiko Angermann*. Please also note that important steps to be performed inside SharePoint are highlighted in *italic*. The same for natural words, those are also highlighted in *italic*. To better find the main techniques to be used in SharePoint, the techniques are written as provided in SharePoint, normaly starting with an upper case letter (e.g. *Site Settings*).

Solution 1: User Management

SharePoint user management is available in *Site Settings*, under the section titled *Users and Permissions*. From the menus included, the administrator of the site can manage permission levels. In addition, the administrator can invite other users to the recent site. The level of access is established by classifying users into different groups, whereby each group can have a different type of permission level. Here, existing groups can be used, or new groups can be created. The solutions presented in this section refer to use cases in which users invited to the recent site are granted full access, and other users are classified into additional user groups granted different degrees of more limited access.

Use Case 1.1: Manage Site Owners

In the *Site Permissions* menu, all types of permission levels are listed. From the site *People and Groups*, the groups that have already been created are listed. The solutions for the exercises are as follows:

- **Exercise 1.1.1—Analyze "SharePoint Permission Levels"**: Seven permission levels exist out of the box (see Figure 5-1): *Full Control* contains all available SharePoint permissions. *Design* allows for viewing, adding, updating, deleting, approving, and customizing. Essentially, this means that users with this type of permission can create lists and libraries but also are allowed to edit existing pages or change the look and feel of the site. *Edit*, allows for lists to be added, edited, and deleted, as well as for users to view, add, update, and delete list items and documents. *Contribute* allows for viewing, adding, updating, and deleting list items and documents. *Read* allows for viewing pages and list items and downloading documents. *Create new subsite* allows for creating subsites. *View Only* allows users to view pages, list items, and documents but does permit editing of any of the preceding. Note that there can be additional permission levels, depending on the version and license of SharePoint.

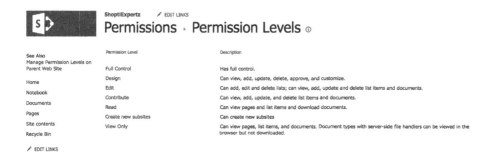

Figure 5-1. Permission levels in SharePoint existing out of the box

- **Exercise 1.1.2—Utilize "SharePoint Permission Levels"**: The owner of the site should be assigned the *Full Control* level. Based on our fictional firm, only the *Operations Manager* and the *Software Manager* should be granted this level of permission. All technicians and experts should be granted the *Read* permission level. All team-leaders should be assigned the *Contribute* permission level. Directors should receive the *Design* permission level.

- **Exercise 1.1.3—Grant Permission to "Owners of ShoptiExperts"**: By navigating to *Site Settings*, users can administrate the different user groups, via the *Site Permissions* menu, under *Users and Permissions*. Here, all groups are listed, and all groups are ascribed a specific level of permission. In the group named *Owners of ShoptiExperts*, the user named *Operations Manager* is listed. Using the *New* button, a new user can be added to this group. By typing the name of the other owner, named *Software Manager*, and clicking *Share*, this user can be classified as the owner of the recent site.

Use Case 1.2: Manage Users Permissions

By navigating to *Site Settings* ➤ *Users and Permissions*, the owner can access the user-management menu named *People and Groups*. The solutions for the exercises are as follows:

- **Exercise 1.2.1—Grant Permissions to "Readers, Designers, and Approvers":** By clicking the corresponding group, an overview appears, wherein all members who are part of this group are listed. The group that allows the permission level for reading is the group named *Visitors*. The group that allows the permission level to design is the group named *Designers*. The group that allows the permission level to approve things is the group named *Approvers*. By clicking the accompanying group, new users can be added (see Figure 5-2).

Figure 5-2. Inviting people to SharePoint user groups

- **Exercise 1.2.2—Grant Permissions to "Contributors":** Until now, no group has been assigned the permission level allowing contributing. The *Create Group* button is used to forward permissions to a new site. A name for the new group to be created can be defined, as well as an optional description. Using the section *Owner*, an owner of the group can be specified. The owner should be the one user having full control of the site, i.e., a site collection administrator. Under the section *Group Settings*, who can view the membership of the group and who can edit the membership of the group can be specified. These settings do not have to be changed. Below, another section is shown that allows for specifying *Membership Requests*. The final section, named *Give Group Permission to this Site*, is provided to assign the group to be created the right type of permission level. Here, the permission level titled *Contribute—Can view, add, update, and delete list items and documents* must be chosen. By clicking the accompanying group, new users can be added, as described in the preceding use case.

Solution 2: Improve Social Networking

For each user, a My Site is created in SharePoint. This can be accessed by clicking the link leading the user to her/his profile, titled *About Me*. Alternatively, by using the *Newsfeed* button in the SharePoint ribbon, the user is forwarded to her/his My Site.

Use Case 2.1: Maintain My Site Profile

By clicking the photo of the My Site owner, or by clicking the *Edit Profile* button, the user is forwarded to a new view, where she/he can edit her/his own profile. Right away, different editable part areas appear as tabs to customize the profile. The different areas and subelements included in these areas can be modified as to which person can view the content. The solutions for the exercises are as follows:

- **Exercise 2.1.1—Maintain "Basic Information"**: From the *Basic Information* tab, the user can enter a personal description with *About Me* (see Figure 5-3). In the *Picture* variable, the user can upload a picture to help others easily recognize the owner of the My Site. In the variable *Ask Me About*, users can maintain tags about topics they can help others with, such as responsibilities or areas of expertise. Each of the variables cannot be adjusted according to who can see the mentioned variable. All variables are visible for every user of the SharePoint site. There are two other variables: *Name* and *Manager* (optional). Both cannot be modified, as they are assigned when setting up the user, or when another user designates the recent owner as the assistant of another person.

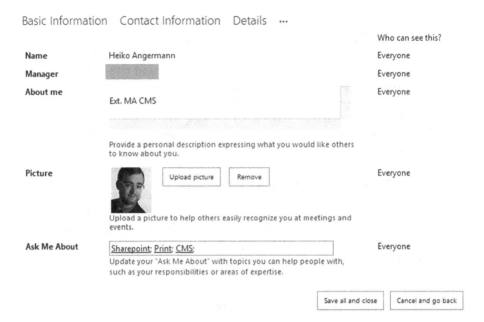

Basic Information   Contact Information   Details   …

		Who can see this?
Name	Heiko Angermann	Everyone
Manager		Everyone
About me	Ext. MA CMS	Everyone

Provide a personal description expressing what you would like others to know about you.

Picture   [Upload picture] [Remove]   Everyone

Upload a picture to help others easily recognize you at meetings and events.

Ask Me About   Sharepoint; Print; CMS;   Everyone

Update your "Ask Me About" with topics you can help people with, such as your responsibilities or areas of expertise.

[Save all and close]   [Cancel and go back]

Figure 5-3. *Editing basic information about a SharePoint user on My Site*

- **Exercise 2.1.2—Maintain "Contact Information"**: In the *Contact Information* tab, the user can maintain information about how she/he can be contacted (see Figure 5-4). The *Work email* variable cannot be edited, as it is provided when setting up the user profile. With the *Mobile phone* variable, the user can enter a contact number of a mobile device. To this number, text messages will be sent, for example, if notification is activated. In the variables following, the user can enter a *Fax* number, a *Home phone* number, her/his *Office Location*, and one *Assistant*. The variable to specifiy the location of the office is baded on taxonomy. Therefore, the user can choose only from locations maintained as a term of a term set. Similar for specifying an asisstant. This is not based on taxonomy, but only existing users can be choosen. The variables *Fax*, *Home phone*, and *Office Location* can be adjusted according to the persons allowed to see this information. The other variables mentioned are visible by *Everyone*.

Basic Information   Contact Information   Details   ...

		Who can see this?
Work email	▮▮▮▮▮▮▮▮▮▮▮	Everyone
Mobile phone	0123/456789	Everyone
	This number will be shown on your profile. Also, it will be used for text message (SMS) alerts.	
Fax	0049123456789	Everyone ▼
Home phone	0123456789	Everyone ▼
Office Location	▮▮▮▮▮▮▮▮	Everyone ▼
	Enter your current location. (e.g. China, Tokyo, West Campus)	
Assistant	▮▮▮▮▮▮▮,	Everyone
	You are only allowed to enter one item.	

Save all and close   Cancel and go back

Figure 5-4. Editing contact information about a SharePoint user on My Site

- **Exercise 2.1.3—Maintain "Details"**: From the *Details* tab, the user can maintain five variables, which are all adjustable according to the persons allowed to see them (see Figure 5-5). In the *Past projects* variable, the user can enter information about previous projects, teams, or groups. In the *Skills* variable, the user can enter, for example, skills that are necessary to perform her/his job. In the *Schools* variable, the user can enter her/his previous academic institutions. Additionally, she/he can use the *Birthday* variable, to enter her/his month and day of birth, and the variable *Interests*, to enter personal and business-related interests. For maintaining the latter variables, tags must be used.

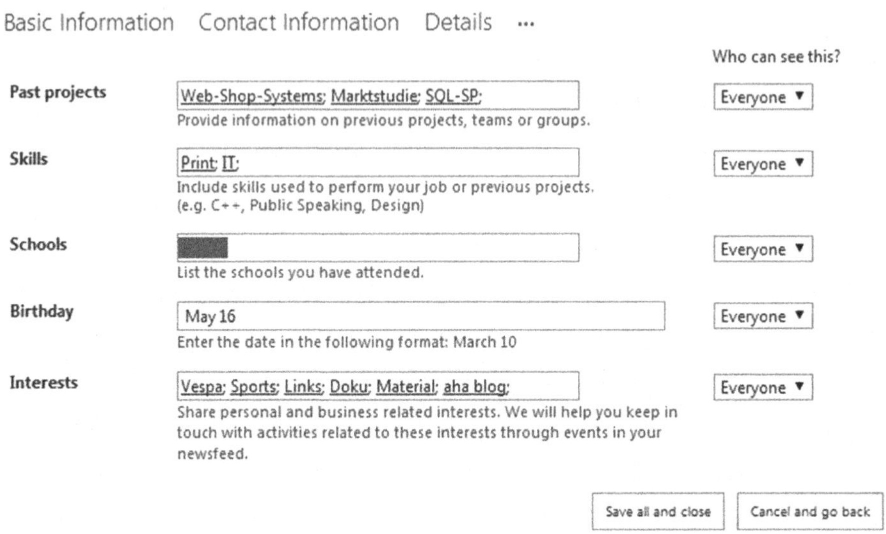

Basic Information   Contact Information   Details   ...

Who can see this?

Past projects	Web-Shop-Systems; Marktstudie; SQL-SP;	Everyone ▼

Provide information on previous projects, teams or groups.

Skills	Print; IT;	Everyone ▼

Include skills used to perform your job or previous projects.
(e.g. C++, Public Speaking, Design)

Schools	▆▆▆	Everyone ▼

List the schools you have attended.

Birthday	May 16	Everyone ▼

Enter the date in the following format: March 10

Interests	Vespa; Sports; Links; Doku; Material; aha blog;	Everyone ▼

Share personal and business related interests. We will help you keep in
touch with activities related to these interests through events in your
newsfeed.

Save all and close   Cancel and go back

Figure 5-5. Editing details about a SharePoint user on My Site

- **Exercise 2.1.4—Maintain "Newsfeed Settings"**: In the *Newsfeed Settings* tab, the user can modify how she/he wants to be informed, and about what she/he should be informed (see Figure 5-6). In the *Followed #Tags* variable, the user can enter the *Enterprise Keywords*, she/he wants to follow. This variable can be adjusted, according to its visibility. From the *Email Notifications* tab, users can specify how and when they should be informed, if there is new content related to one of the above-maintained keywords. Using the *People I follow* variable, the user can decide if other users are permitted to see the people they are following. Finally, using the variable *Activities I want to share in my newsfeed*, users can specify what they want to share. After editing the profile using the four tabs, the changes must be confirmed, by clicking the *Save all and close* button.

Basic Information   Contact Information   Newsfeed Settings   ⋯

		Who can see this?
Followed #Tags	#CMS; #Übung; #Vorlesung;	Everyone ▼
	Stay up-to-date on topics that interest you by following #tags. Posts with these #tags will show up in your newsfeed.	
Email Notifications	☑ Someone has started following me	
	☑ Suggestions for people and keywords I might be interested in	
	☑ Someone has mentioned me	
	☑ Someone replied to a conversation that I started	
	☑ Someone replied to a conversation that I replied to	
	☑ Someone replied to my community discussion post	
	Pick what email notifications you want to get.	
People I follow	☑ Allow others to see the people you're following and the people following you when they view your profile.	Everyone
Activities I want to share in my newsfeed	☑ Share all of them ⓘ	Everyone
	☑ Following a person	
	☑ Following a document or site	
	☑ Following a tag	
	☑ Tagging an item	
	☑ Birthday celebration	
	☑ Job title change	
	☑ Workplace anniversary	
	☑ Updating your "Ask Me About"	
	☑ Posting on a note board	
	☑ Liking or rating something	
	☑ New blog post	
	☑ Participation in communities	
	Pick the activities you want to tell people about.	

Save all and close   Cancel and go back

Figure 5-6. Editing newsfeed settings of a SharePoint user on My Site

- **Exercise 2.1.5—Save Profile and Connect**: In the upper right corner of My Site, the headlines *People*, *Documents*, *Sites*, and *Tags* appear. All four list which artifacts (people, documents, etc.) the recent user is following. Using the *People* button, the user is navigated to an overview showing all people the user is following. Using the text box, and the button *Follow*, the user can add multiple users who also have access to the recent SharePoint site. Those users are recognized by their e-mail address or their name. The added users are the followers of the My Site owner, i.e., the people she/he is now connected with.

Use Case 2.2: My Site Features

In addition to those that maintain a user's personal profile, My Site provides additional features. In the following use case, the creation of a blog is considered, including a document management library and the customization of links. The solutions for the exercises are as follows:

- **Exercise 2.2.1—Create a "Blog"**: In the local navigation of the newsfeed environment, the *Blog* link is already integrated. After clicking the link, the user is forwarded to her/his own blog. Here, it is shown that different categories of blog entries already exist. However, using the *Blog tools* button, the user is forwarded to a site wherein she/he can remove the existing categories and also create new categories as list items. Using *Blog tools* again, the user can *Create a post*, i.e., a blog post. These posts can be classified into the categories entered in the *Category* variable in the previous step (see Figure 5-7). Using the *Title* variable, which is mandatory, the author can write a title for the post. Using the *Body* variable, the user can write the text of the post message. Finally, the mandatory variable *Published*, lets the author of the recent post specify when the blog entry should be published (see Figure 5-8).

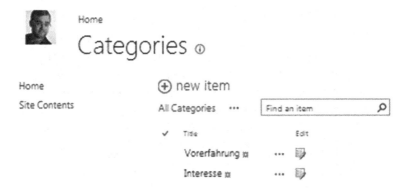

Figure 5-7. Managing categories for a blog post

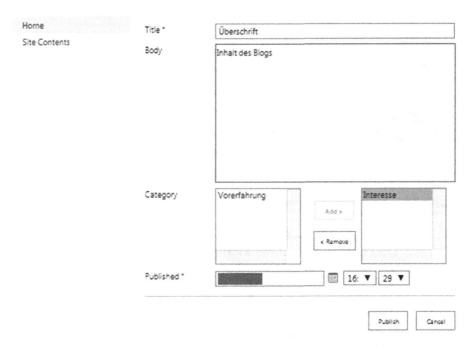

Figure 5-8. Creating a blog item with a title, body, category, and date of publication

- **Exercise 2.2.2—Manage "Documents":** In each SharePoint My Site, the SkyDrive (also named OneDrive) functionality is already included. In SharePoint 2016, this functionality is available via the already integrated app named *Documents* (shown in Figure 5-9). This gives every user a centralized place for storing and managing documents. The documents can be structured into folders, and the documents and folders can be shared with other users. In addition, documents that the owner of the My Site is following are shown, and workflows can be added to the documents. By default, the *Shared with Everyone* folder exists, which means that every document stored inside this folder is visible to every user. Using the Files ribbon, the user can create a *New Folder* by specifying its name. Using the *Shared With* button, the owner can precisely specify who is allowed to see the documents being stored inside this folder. The added persons are notified by e-mail. Inside the folder (also outside folders), a *New Document* can be added. Using the *Share* function, the document can also be released to people who do not have access to the global folder.

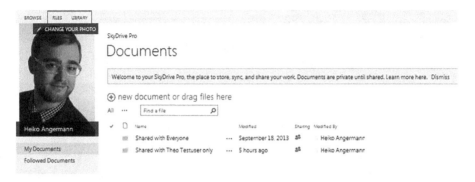

Figure 5-9. OneDrive feature being integrated on the SharePoint My Site

- **Exercise 2.2.3—Customize "Links"**: Using the *Edit Links* button, part of the local navigation of My Site, the user can quickly edit the shown links and also add new links to this navigation. The pages to be added can be specified according the *Text to display* and according to the *Address*, meaning that the URL of the site is to be included as a link (see Figure 5-10).

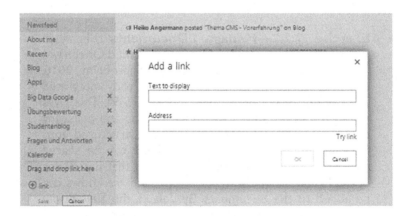

Figure 5-10. Adding links to the user interface of the SharePoint My Site

Solution 3: Customize Look and Feel

Very often, the look and feel of SharePoint must be customized. This is referred to by the term SharePoint branding. The branding can be performed on different levels, depending on the budget. If SharePoint is only used as an intranet, the techniques provided out of the box are often enough to customize the look and feel. In SharePoint, this type of customizing can be performed as part of the *Site Settings*, from the *Look and Feel* menu.

Use Case 3.1: Using and Customizing Themes

The first steps are to customize the basic information shown to the users: title of the site and the logo. In addition, what are called themes are used. These allow quick customization of the application according to a color palette more appropriate to an enterprise's corporate identity. The solutions for the exercises are as follows:

- **Exercise 3.1.1—Change "Title, description, and logo"**: By navigating to the *Site Settings* page, all possible settings appear. In the top right of this site, the *Look and Feel* menu appears. By clicking the submenu *Title, description, and logo*, a new site appears (see Figure 5-11). Here, the user can specify the *Title* of the SharePoint site, including a *Description* of it. Below, using *Insert Logo*, a logo can be uploaded to SharePoint. Here, the user can upload a new logo, or use a logo already uploaded to SharePoint.

Site Settings ▸ Title, Description, and Logo

Title and Description
Type a title and description for your site.

Title:

ShoptiExpertz

Description:

Logo and Description
Associate a logo with this site. Add an optional description for the image. Note: If the file location has a local relative address, for example, /_layouts/images/logo.gif, you must copy the graphics file to that location on each front-end Web server.

Insert Logo:
FROM COMPUTER | FROM SHAREPOINT

Enter a description (used as alternative text for the picture):

Web Site Address
Users can navigate to your site by typing the Web site address (URL) into their browser. You can enter the last part of the address. You should keep it short and easy to remember.

For example,
https://shoptiexpertz.sharepoint.com/sitename

URL name:
https://shoptiexpertz.sharepoint.com/ shoptiexpertz

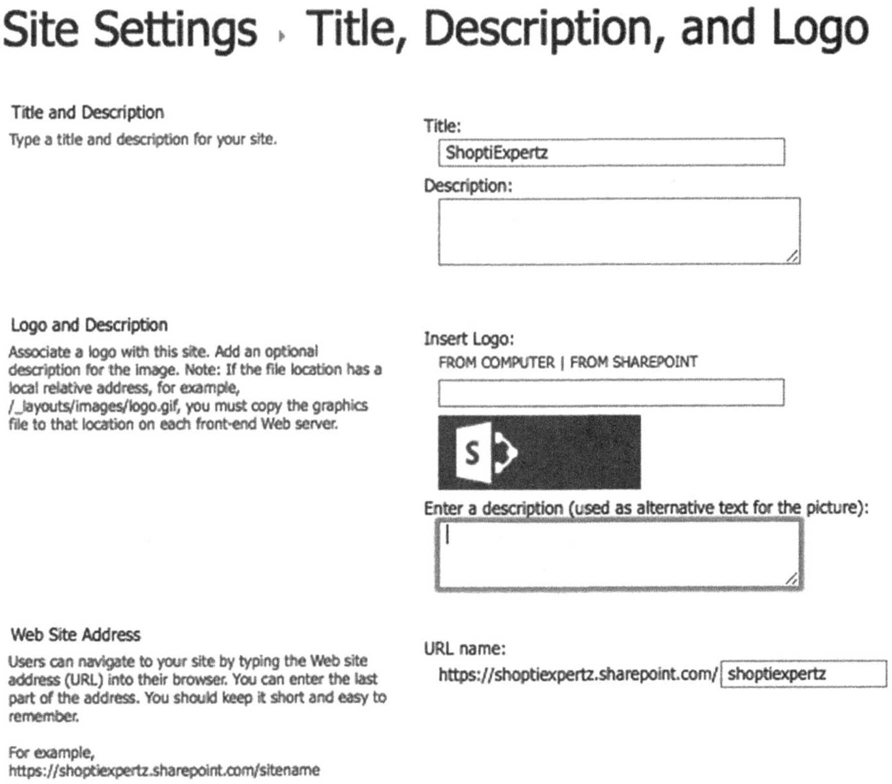

Figure 5-11. Editing the title, description, and logo of the SharePoint site

- **Exercise 3.1.2—Change "Master Page"**: Navigating to *Site Settings*, the *Look and Feel* menu appears at the top right. The section allowing editing the master page does not appear yet. To overcome this, the *SharePoint Server Publishing Infrastructure* and *SharePoint Server Publishing* features must be activated. To do so, the *Site collection features* submenu of the *Site Collection Administration* menu must be chosen. A site appears in which the previously mentioned feature can be activated (see Figure 5-12). Afterward, the *Manage site features* submenu of the *Site Actions* menu must be chosen. Here, the *SharePoint Server Publishing* feature must be activated (see Figure 5-13). Afterward, the *Master page* submenu appears below the *Look and Feel* menu. On clicking this submenu, a new site appears. Here, two main sections appear (see Figure 5-14). In the first section, the *Site Master Page* can be defined. This means that the master page, which is used by all sites and visible to every user, is defined. In the second section, the *System Master Page* can be defined. This means that the master page, which is used by all sites and includes the techniques used to administrate the site, is defined. In both sections, the user can choose two existing master pages, *Seattle* and *Oslo*, by using a drop-down menu. Each section further includes two click boxes. In the first box, the user can choose whether the page should be inherited from its parent site, or vice versa. The first option is grayed out, as it is only possible to inherit from parent sites, if you are not customizing the top-level site of your SharePoint environment. In addition, a further click box appears below the drop-down menu in the two sections, where it can be specified if the subsites must be reset, inheriting this master page's setting(s). After clicking *OK* and looking at the other browser tab, it becomes obvious that the navigation has completely changed. Now, the global navigation appears at the top, and the top navigation does not exist anymore.

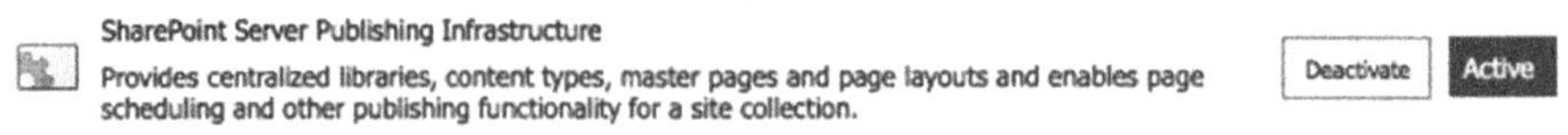

SharePoint Server Publishing Infrastructure

Provides centralized libraries, content types, master pages and page layouts and enables page scheduling and other publishing functionality for a site collection.

Deactivate   Active

Figure 5-12. *Activating the SharePoint feature to enable the publishing infrastructure*

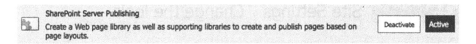

Figure 5-13. Activating the SharePoint feature to enable publishing techniques

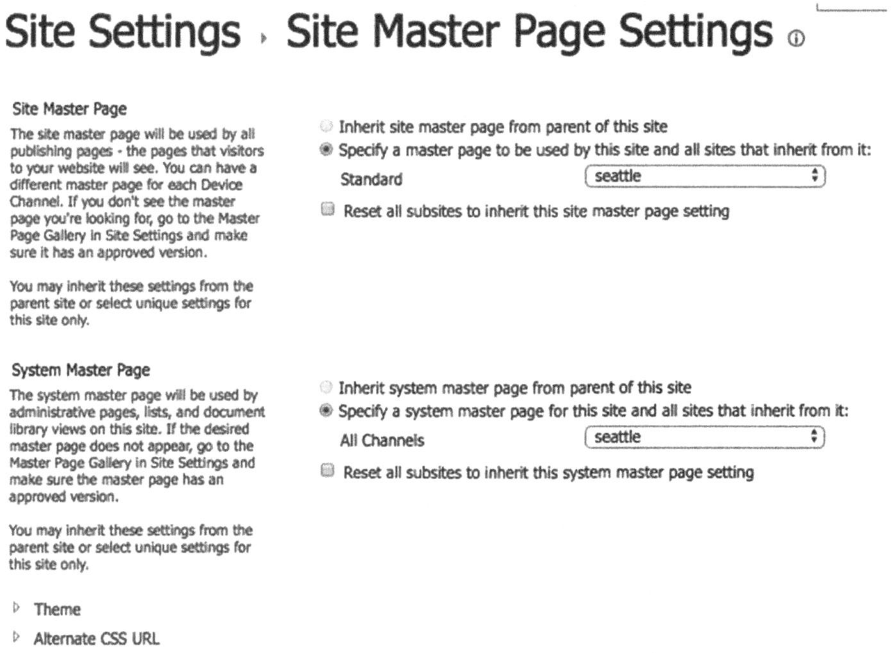

Site Settings ⟩ Site Master Page Settings ⓘ

Site Master Page

The site master page will be used by all publishing pages - the pages that visitors to your website will see. You can have a different master page for each Device Channel. If you don't see the master page you're looking for, go to the Master Page Gallery in Site Settings and make sure it has an approved version.

You may inherit these settings from the parent site or select unique settings for this site only.

○ Inherit site master page from parent of this site
● Specify a master page to be used by this site and all sites that inherit from it:
    Standard   [seattle   ‡]

☐ Reset all subsites to inherit this site master page setting

System Master Page

The system master page will be used by administrative pages, lists, and document library views on this site. If the desired master page does not appear, go to the Master Page Gallery in Site Settings and make sure the master page has an approved version.

You may inherit these settings from the parent site or select unique settings for this site only.

○ Inherit system master page from parent of this site
● Specify a system master page for this site and all sites that inherit from it:
    All Channels   [seattle   ‡]

☐ Reset all subsites to inherit this system master page setting

▷ Theme
▷ Alternate CSS URL

Figure 5-14. Site for editing the utilized master page

- **Exercise 3.1.3—Customize "Change the Look":** Navigating to *Site Settings*, the *Look and Feel* menu appears, including its *Change the look* submenu. After clicking this submenu, 18 styles are shown. The templates differ according to color and the navigations and fonts used. After clicking one template, a new site appears (see Figure 5-15). Here, the user can change the image shown on the SharePoint site, a new color palette can be chosen (*Colors*), a *Site layout* can be defined (i.e., the master page), and the utilized *Fonts* can be chosen. After choosing the template *Orange*, *Oslo* as layout, and *Century Gothic* as font, the SharePoint site takes on a look and feel more similar to those required by the firm.

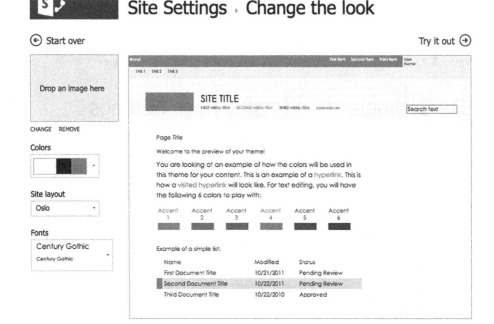

Figure 5-15. Site for editing the chosen theme

Use Case 3.2: Customizing Navigation and Links

Apart from using a more fitting theme, the structure of the content to be displayed on the sites and pages can be customized with out of the box techniques. The most important element here is the navigation, as this is the first element that helps users find the desired place and data. The solutions for the exercises are as follows:

- **Exercise 3.2.1—Customize "Page Layouts":** Navigating to the tile gear, a new menu pops up, including *Add a page*. After clicking on this button, a new window pops up again. Here, the user must specify a name for the new page to be created, using the variable *Give it a name*. After clicking *OK*, the user is forwarded to the new page, which is only recently visible to the user who created this page. The *Page Layout* menu is part of the *Page* menu (see Figure 5-16). For choosing the page layout named *Splash*, the user must scroll down to the drop-down menu showing all page layouts.

Figure 5-16. Choosing a page layout to be used by a page

- **Exercise 3.2.2—Customize "Homepage"**: At the top of the page, the name of the page is shown. Below, a box appears, in which this title can be modified (see Figure 5-17). Below the title, another box is shown, named *Page Image*. Here, the user can insert a picture from SharePoint. If the image does not already exist in SharePoint, the image can also be uploaded from another storage place. The *Preview* menu is part of the *Page* menu. After clicking this button, the site is shown in preview; however, not much has changed, as each part can still be edited. The button to define this page as a home page is named *Make Homepage*.

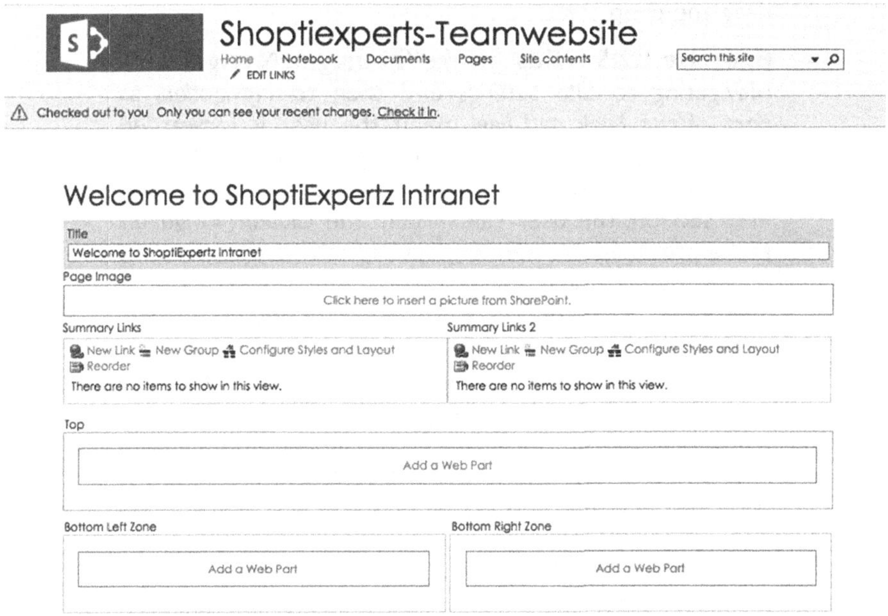

Figure 5-17. Customizing a single page in SharePoint

- **Exercise 3.2.3—Publish "Homepage"**: Until now, the site is not yet available, as it is not yet checked-in (Figure 5-18). Only the creator of this page can see it. After saving the changes, the *Publish* button should be clicked. Finally, the page is now visible to every user, and it is the home page of the site.

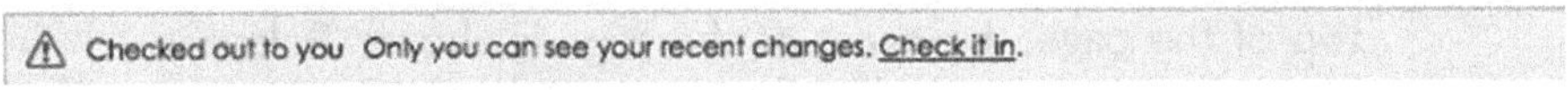

⚠ Checked out to you Only you can see your recent changes. Check it in.

Figure 5-18. *Publishing a single page in SharePoint*

- **Exercise 3.2.4—Customize "Links"**: After navigating to the home page created in the preceding step, the user can *Edit Links* (possible on each page, if the user has the required permissions). Using this button, a new pop-up appears, with which the user can specify a *Title* of the navigation element to be included and an *Address*, meaning the URL. The functionality of the link can be tested by using *Try Link*. All links can be moved in the navigation by drag and drop.

- **Exercise 3.2.5—Customize "Managed Navigation"**: Navigating to *Site Settings* and then to *Navigation*, as part of the *Look and Feel* menu, the user is forwarded to a new page on which to change *Navigation Settings* (see Figure 5-19). Here, different sections appear. In the first section, the user can modify the *Global Navigation*. More precisely, the user can specify the navigation items to display in global navigation for the SharePoint site. The second section has the same aim, but for *Current Navigation*. In both sections, the user can define whether to *Display the same navigation items as the parent site* (only for subsites; otherwise, grayed out), select *Managed Navigation*, or *Structural Navigation*. In addition, in both sections, the user can specify if *Structural Navigation* is activated, whether to *Show subsites*, and whether to *Show pages*. If *Structural Navigation* is chosen, the user can define whether the navigation should *Sort automatically* or *Sort manually*. Using the section below, *Structural Navigation: Editing and Sorting*, the navigation can be sorted manually. Here, new links can be added by using *Add Link*. New headings can be added by using *Add Heading* (placeholder links), which can be defined as to whether a page should be hidden, links can be edited, and the position of the pages can be changed. For the latter, the buttons *Move Up* and *Move Down* should be used. Those also allow links to be nested in other links or headings, resulting in child-parent relationships. The last section defines if the ribbon of the SharePoint site should be shown or not (*Show and Hide Ribbon*).

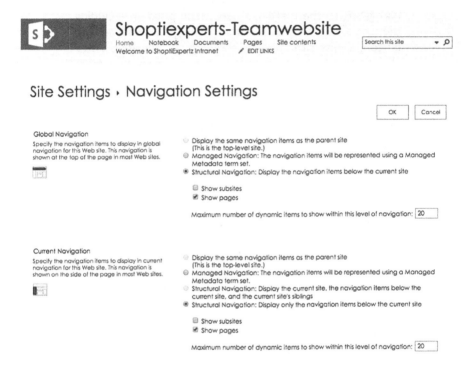

Figure 5-19. Customizing the navigation settings to be used by a SharePoint site

Solution 4: Integrate Applications

For allowing specific functionalities for storing and managing data, SharePoint provides apps. Different apps fall into three main categories: list, library, and calendar. The two former types of applications are most often used and customized.

Use Case 4.1: Adding and Customizing Lists

Adding a list can be achieved by navigating to *Site Contents*. Here, all the existing apps are listed. For customizing a list, columns are the main element to be adapted according to an enterprise's requirements. The solutions for the exercises are as follows:

- **Exercise 4.1.1—Understand "Custom List"**: Navigating to the tilegear, a new menu pops up, including the *Site Contents* menu. After clicking the *Add an App* button, a new site appears, showing all *Your Apps*. After clicking the *Custom List* button, a pop up appears from which a *Name* for the list to be created can be picked and then confirmed (see Figure 5-20). The button *List* allows the following operations to be performed: *View Format, Manage Views, Tags and Notes, Share & Track, Connect & Export, Customize List*, and *Settings*. Under *View Format*, the user can *Quick Edit* the view. Using *Manage Views*, a new view can be created (*Create View*), the recent view can be modified (*Modify View*), a new column can be added to the recent view (*Create Column*), and the *Current View* can be chosen. Under *Tags and Notes*, the *Enterprise Keywords* for the list can be modified. *Share & Track* allows users to *E-mail a Link*, including the link of the recent list, to other users and to modify *RSS Feed*. *Connect & Export* exports the list to Excel (*Export to Excel*). *Customize List* includes buttons to modify *Form Web Parts*; to *Edit List*, using Microsoft SharePoint Designer; and to add a *New Quick Step*. Finally, *Settings* navigates the user to the *List Settings*, which is the most important setting for the list. Additionally, the user can edit the share settings (*Shared With*) and modify *Workflow Settings*. Other buttons exist but are grayed out, depending on the configuration of the SharePoint farm. The *Items* button allows *New* creations. All other options in both buttons (*Items* and *List*) are recently grayed out; however, they are no longer grayed out if content is added to the list, by creating a *New Folder* to *Manage* the existing items, including *View Item, Edit Item, Version History, Shared With*, and *Delete Item*. Under *Actions*, a new file can be attached to a list item (*Attach File*). Under *Tags and Notes*, the *Enterprise Keywords* used for a recent item can be modified. And, finally, under *Workflows*, buttons are included to start workflows or, if the approval workflow is already started, the list item can be directly approved or rejected with the *Approve/Reject* button.

Figure 5-20. Adding a list application to a SharePoint site

- **Exercise 4.1.2—Create "Columns"**: A new column can be created with the *List* button and by clicking *Create Column*. Afterward, a pop up appears, from which the new column to be created can be specified. In the first section, *Name and Type*, the name of the column (*Column name*) can be specified, as well as the type of the column (see Figure 5-21). Here, the type can be *Single line of text*, meaning a string; *Multiple lines of text*, meaning a larger string; *Choice*, resulting in a click box; *Number*, meaning an integer value; *Currency*; *Date and Time*; *Lookup*, meaning a lookup to already existing information; *Yes/No*, meaning a boolean value; *Person or Group*, whereby a SharePoint user or group can be added to the list item; *Hyperlink or Picture*, meaning to maintain an URL leading to a page or figure; *Calculated*, meaning to maintain a formula automatically resulting a value; *Task Outcome*; *External Data*, meaning to link the list item to data outside of SharePoint; and *Managed Metadata*, meaning to specify a term for the recent list item. In the section below, *Additional Column Settings* can be configured. These include specifying a *Description* for the column: if it is required that the column contain information, if unique values must be enforced, what the maximum number of characters is, and the default value for the column. After clicking *OK*, the column is asserted to the recent view. To modify the column, the user must click the *Modify View* button, before the side to *Edit View* appears. In the first section of the side, *Name* can be edited. Below, the modifications for the columns can be performed. Each column is listed by its *Column Name* and can be specified, according to whether it has to be shown. In addition, a drop-down menu is shown for all columns, in which the position can be specified. Other sections exist to sort the list items. Also, to the previously mentioned sections (functions), the list can include a filter; the view can be switched to a tabular view; items can be grouped; totals can be modified; the style can be adjusted; folders can be specified; an item limit can be specified; and the view can be adjusted for mobile display.

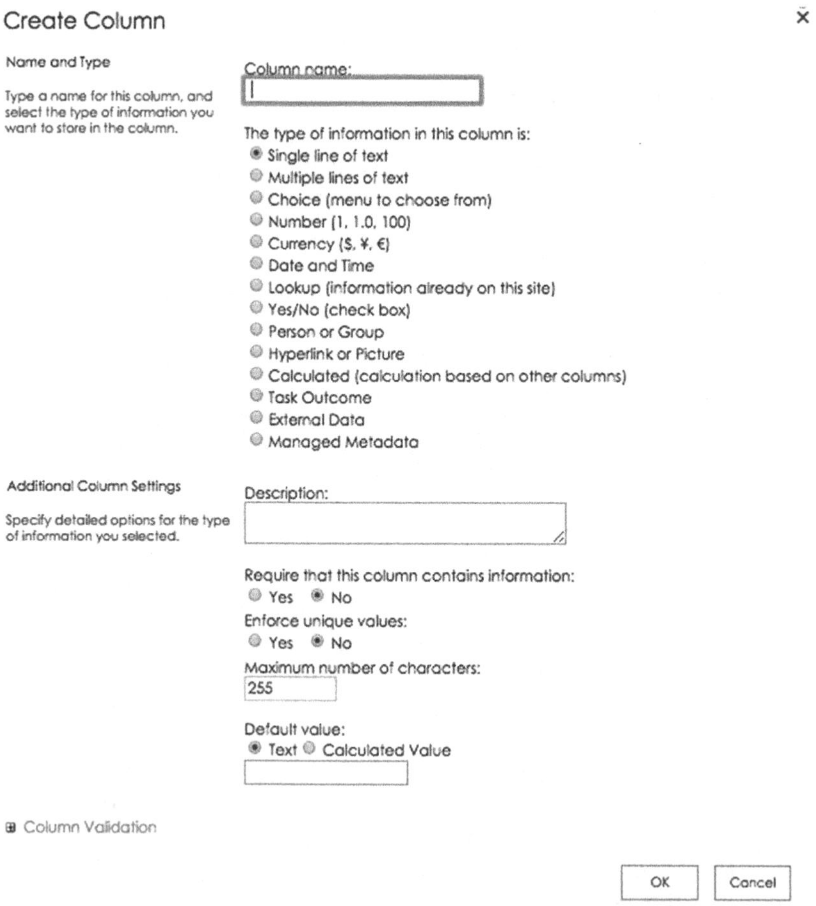

Create Column   ×

Name and Type

Type a name for this column, and select the type of information you want to store in the column.

Column name:

The type of information in this column is:
- ● Single line of text
- ○ Multiple lines of text
- ○ Choice (menu to choose from)
- ○ Number (1, 1.0, 100)
- ○ Currency ($, ¥, €)
- ○ Date and Time
- ○ Lookup (information already on this site)
- ○ Yes/No (check box)
- ○ Person or Group
- ○ Hyperlink or Picture
- ○ Calculated (calculation based on other columns)
- ○ Task Outcome
- ○ External Data
- ○ Managed Metadata

Additional Column Settings

Specify detailed options for the type of information you selected.

Description:

Require that this column contains information:
○ Yes ● No

Enforce unique values:
○ Yes ● No

Maximum number of characters:
255

Default value:
● Text ○ Calculated Value

⊞ Column Validation

OK   Cancel

Figure 5-21. *Adding a single column to a SharePoint list application*

- **Exercise 4.1.3—Create "Metadata Columns"**: A new column can be created using the *List* button and clicking *Create Column*. Afterward, a pop up appears, in which the new column to be created can be specified. In the first section, *Name and Type*, the name has to be defined. As type, *Managed Metadata* must be chosen. For this type, a *Description* can be maintained, using the section *Additional Column Settings*. If the recent column should be a *Multiple Value field*, this can be specified in the section below, using the check box *Allow multiple values*. In the *Display format* section, whether the complete path of a term (including subterms) should be displayed in this column, or only the actual chosen term, can be specified. The most important section of this type of column is *Term Set Settings*. Here, the user can finally specify the term (taxonomy) being used for this column. If the column should use the date of an existing taxonomy, the check box *Use a managed term set* should be chosen; otherwise, the user can create a new taxonomy using *"Customize your term set,"* illustrated in Figure 5-22. Clicking this box, a term is created as a root concept, having the same name as the name of the column. Clicking on the root concept, and using *Create Term*, creates a term that is a sub concept of the root concept. Here, the user can define a name for the term to be created. Clicking the recently created term, the user can also create a term for this term, that is, a sub concept of the concept or a sub concept of the root concept. Through this, endless hierarchies can be simulated in SharePoint, performing as term sets of the taxonomy. It also can be specified if fill-in options should be supported. Additionally, a default term can be specified below, before finally creating this type of column by pressing *OK*.

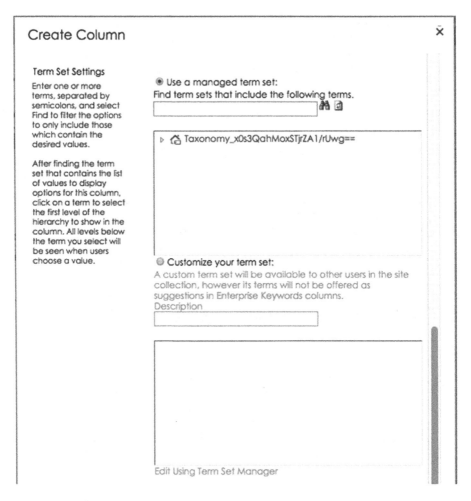

Figure 5-22. *Specifying/adding a term set to a column of type managed metadata*

- **Exercise 4.1.4—Create "Person Columns 1"**: The final required column can be created using the *List* button again and clicking *Create Column*. Afterward, a pop up appears, from which the new column to be created can be specified. In the first section, *Name and Type*, again, the *Column name* and *Column Type* can be specified. In contrast to the preceding exercise, now the column type should be *Person or Group*. The section below named *Additional Column Settings* has different options than the other column types. A *Description* can be defined. This section also lets the user specify if this column should require information, enforce unique values is required, and if multiple values are allowed in this column. Below (*Allow selection of*), whether the column should contain *People Only* or *People and Groups* can be specified. In addition, the user can specify whether any user can be input in this column, or if only users from a specific SharePoint group can be input. Finally, how the person or group should be displayed in this column can be specified.

- **Exercise 4.1.5—Create "Custom Views"**: A completely new view for a list can be created by using the *Create View* button shown under the *List* ribbon. After clicking this button, the user is forwarded to a new site, from which she/he can choose different types of *View Type*. The *Standard View* is one of several different view types, including: *Calendar View, Datasheet View, Gantt View*, and *Custom View in SharePoint Designer*. Using the *Name* section, the name of the view to be created can be entered. In addition, the user can specify if she/he wants to *Create a Personal View* or *Create a Public View*, as opposed to all users having access to this list. This option is available in the section named *Audience*. Most important for this exercise is the *Columns* section. Here, it can be indicated that the cited columns should be displayed, and the position for each column can be modified.

Use Case 4.2: Adding and Customizing Libraries

Adding a library can be performed when navigating to *Site Contents*. For customizing a library, columns are the main element that can be adapted according to an enterprise's needs. The solutions for the exercises are as follows:

- **Exercise 4.2.1—Understand "Document Library"**: Navigating to the tilegear, a new menu pops up, including the *Site Contents* menu. After clicking this menu, a new site appears, listing the *Site Contents*, including *Lists, Libraries, and other Apps*. After clicking the *Add an App* button, a new site appears, showing all apps. After clicking the button *Document Library*, a pop up appears, from which a *Name* can be picked for the library to be created and then confirmed with *OK* (see preceding Figure 5-23). The *Library* button allows the following operations: *View Format, Manage Views, Tags and Notes, Share & Track, Connect & Export, Customize Library*, and *Settings*. Under *View Format*, the user can *Quick Edit* the view. Using *Manage*

Views, a new view can be created (*Create View*), the recent view can be modified (*Modify View*), a new column can be added to the recent view (*Create Column*), and the *Current View* can be chosen. Under *Tags and Notes*, the *Enterprise Keywords* for the list can be modified. *Share & Track* allows users to *E-mail a Link*, including the link of the recent list, to other users and, to modify *RSS Feed*. *Connect & Export* facilitates exporting the list to Excel (*Export to Excel*). *Customize Library* includes buttons to modify *Form Web Parts*, to *Edit Library using Microsoft SharePoint Designer*, and to add a *New Quick Step*. Finally, *Settings* navigates the user to *Library Settings*, which is the most important setting for the list. Additionally, the user can edit the share settings (*Shared With*) and modify *Workflow Settings*. Other buttons exist but are grayed out. Those depend on the configuration of the SharePoint farm. The *Files* button allows the following operations to be performed: *Create New* document, *Open & Check Out*, *Manage documents*, *Share & Track* documents, manage *Copies*, as well as specify *Workflows* and administrate *Tags and Notes*. For new lists, only the *New* menu is not grayed out.

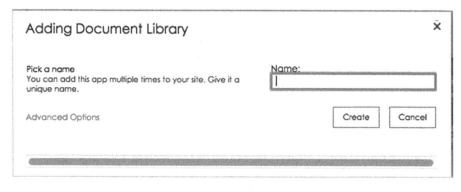

Figure 5-23. Adding a library application to a SharePoint site

- **Exercise 4.2.2—Create "Person Columns 2"**: A new column can be created using the *Library* button and clicking *Create Column*. Afterward, a pop up appears, from which the new column to be created can be specified. In the first section, *Name and Type*, the name of the column (*Column name*) and its type can be specified. The type can be a *Single line of text*, meaning a string; *Multiple lines of text*, meaning a larger string; *Choice*, resulting in a click box; *Number*, meaning an integer value; *Currency*; *Date and Time*;

Lookup, meaning a lookup to already existing information; *Yes/No*, meaning a boolean value; *Person or Group*, from which a SharePoint user or group can be added to the list item; *Hyperlink or Picture*, meaning to maintain a URL leading to a page or figure; *Calculated*, meaning to maintain a formula automatically resulting in a value; *Task Outcome*; *External Data*, meaning to link the list item to data outside of SharePoint; and *Managed Metadata*, meaning to specify a term for the recent list item. Logically, the column to be created should be of the type *Person or Group*. In the section below, *Additional Column Settings* can be performed. This includes specifying a *Description* for the column, if it is required that this column contain information, if unique values must be enforced, if multiple selections are allowed, and if the column is limited to a specific user group, or if all users can be inserted in this column. In addition, it can be specified to whom the column should be shown. After clicking *OK*, the column is asserted to the library. The setting *Enterprise Keyword* can be specified, using *Library Settings* and going to *Enterprise Metadata and Keywords Settings*. In the first section, named *Add Enterprise Keywords*, it can be specified if an *Enterprise Keywords* column should be asserted to the library. In the section below named *Metadata Publishing*, it can be specified if the keywords should be saved as social tags. Finally, the accompanying column, which is already added to the library, must be visible in the recent view. To ensure this, *Modify View* must be used, which leads to the page named *Edit View*. In the second section, named *Columns*, the accompanying column can be added to the view named *Enterprise Keywords*.

- **Exercise 4.2.3—Create "Metadata Columns"**: All the mentioned metadata columns are already available for the library. However, those must be added to the recent view. To do this, *Modify View* must be used, which leads to the page named *Edit View*. In the second section, named *Columns*, the accompanying columns can be added to the view, which are named *Check In Comment*, *Created*, *Created By*, *Edit*, and *Version*.

- **Exercise 4.2.4—Create "Personal View"**: To create a view that only shows documents uploaded by oneself, the view must be modified. The page that allows for modifying the view is available by enlarging the ribbon named *Library* and clicking *Modify View*. Afterward, the user is forwarded to the *Edit view* page. Using the *Filter* section, different settings to filter content are provided. By default, the filter is able to *Show all items in this view*. This must be changed to *Show items only when the following is true*. Afterward, the column *Consultant* can be chosen, using the functions *Show the items when column* ➤ *Consultant* ➤ *is equal to* ➤ *Operations Manager*. To create another view, where only content from the team members is shown, the *Create View* button must be clicked. Afterward, the page *View Type* appears. Here, five views are displayed. To create the list, as required, the view type *Standard View* has to be clicked, which forwards the user to the page *Create View*. Using the *Name* section of the *Create View* site, the name of the view to be created, which is *Operations Management*, can be maintained. In addition, the user can specify if she/he wants to *Create a Personal View* or to *Create a Public View*, as opposed to all users having access to this list. This option is available in the section named *Audience*. As the view is to be shared by all team members, we *Create a Public View* (see Figure 5-24). To filter for documents only uploaded by operative management staff, the section named *Filter* must be used. Again, the different names of the team members must be filtered, as described previously. Filtering for various team members requires that multiple filters be created. This means that each person must be specified, and the filters work together using *Or*. More convenient would be to filter for groups instead. This allows, in addition, that the filter would be more dynamic, for example, to accommodate new team members or to remove members who have left the team. To manage this, a group must be created in advance, so that the filter can perform on the group level instead.

Settings ▸ Create View

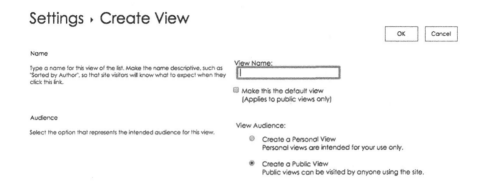

| | OK | Cancel |

Name

Type a name for this view of the list. Make the name descriptive, such as "Sorted by Author", so that site visitors will know what to expect when they click this link.

View Name:

☐ Make this the default view
(Applies to public views only)

Audience

Select the option that represents the intended audience for this view.

View Audience:

○ Create a Personal View
Personal views are intended for your use only.

◉ Create a Public View
Public views can be visited by anyone using the site.

Figure 5-24. Creating a customized view for a SharePoint application

Use Case 4.3: Adding Workflows to Applications

Workflows help to automatize and standardize processes. In SharePoint, workflows can be activated (added) to any type of app. The different workflows that are available out of the box can be further customized. The solutions for the exercises are as follows:

- **Exercise 4.3.1—Activate "Workflows"**: When installing SharePoint from scratch, some features are not automatically activated. The reason is that the features are chosen according to the template used for a site-collection or subsite. To activate the feature named *Workflows*, the user has to navigate to the *Site Settings, Site Collection Administration*, and, finally, *Site Collection Features*. A new page, then appears. Here, all features performing on the site level are listed. Each feature has a status, either *Deactivate* or *Active*. Logically, clicking the latter mentioned button, shown in Figure 5-25, can activate the required feature.

Workflows
Aggregated set of out-of-box workflow features provided by SharePoint.

| Deactivate | Active |

Figure 5-25. Activating the workflows feature

- **Exercise 4.3.2—Manage "Approval Workflow"**: By clicking on *Site Contents*, an overview of all applications already created are listed, including the *Document Library*. To add a workflow, the *Library* ribbon must be enlarged, before clicking Workflow Settings. Afterward, a new page with the same name appears, including the link to the page named *Add a workflow*. On this page, the first section, *Workflow*, allows selection from an existing workflow template (*Select a workflow template*), illustrated in Figure 5-26. Here, five workflow templates are listed: *Disposition approval, Three State, Collect Feedback, Approval*, and *Collect signature*. For each workflow template, a description is shown. In the section below, the user can enter a unique name for the workflow to be created. The section below named *Task List* must be used to collect all tasks required to perform the workflow. In this list, all workflow tasks for the responsible persons are listed. There is another section, named *History List*. Here, a list can be specified to summarize all steps occurring during performance of the workflow for a single item. The final section, named *Start Options*, provides different functionalities to specify when the workflow should be started.

Settings ▸ Add a Workflow
Workflow Details

Workflow

Select a workflow to add to this document library. If a workflow is missing from the list, your site administrator may have to publish or activate it

Select a workflow template:
- *Drei Status
- *Feedback sammeln - SharePoint 2010
- *Genehmigung - SharePoint 2010
- *Signaturerfassung - SharePoint 2010

Description:
Leitet ein Dokument zur Genehmigung weiter. Genehmigende Personen können das Dokument genehmigen oder ablehnen, die Genehmigungsaufgabe einer anderen Person zuweisen oder aber Änderungen am Dokument anfordern.

*Denotes a SharePoint 2010 template.

Name

Enter a name for this workflow. The name will be used to identify this workflow to users of this document library.

Enter a unique name for this workflow:

Task List

Select the name of the task list to use with this workflow, or create a new one.

Select a task list:
Workflowaufgaben

Description:
This system library was created by the Publishing feature to store workflow tasks that are created in this site.

History List

Select the name of the history list to use with this workflow, or create a new one.

Select a history list:
Workflow History (new)

Description:
This workflow will use a new history list.

Start Options

Specify how this workflow can be started.

☑ Allow this workflow to be manually started by an authenticated user with Edit Item permissions.
    ☐ Require Manage Lists Permissions to start the workflow.

☐ Start this workflow to approve publishing a major version of an item.

☐ Creating a new item will start this workflow.

☐ Changing an item will start this workflow.

Figure 5-26. Adding a workflow to a SharePoint application

Solution 5: Using Metadata Techniques

In SharePoint, two types of metadata techniques exist: taxonomy, and folksonomy. In SharePoint, metadata can be added to various content types. Often, the formal technique is used to classify documents or to hierarchically organize something, e.g., departments. The informal technique is often used in addition to the formal technique, for example, to further describe information or data.

Use Case 5.1: Using Managed Metadata Techniques

Managed Metadata is often used in libraries or lists to formally classify items or documents. To do so, a column of this type must be added to an application. The solutions for the exercises are as follows:

- **Exercise 5.1.1—Add "Managed Metadata Document Library"**: A new column can be created using the *Library* button and clicking *Create Column*. Afterward, a pop up appears, from which the new column to be created can be specified. In the first section, *Name and Type*, the name of the column (*Column name*), which is *Taxonomy*, can be specified, as can the type of the column, which is *Managed Metadata*. To add the new column to the default view, the accompanying check box has to be active.

- **Exercise 5.1.2—Customize "Term Set"**: In the section named *Term Set Settings*, the taxonomy to be chosen for this column can be specified. Here, either an already existing taxonomy can be used (*Use a managed term set*), or a new taxonomy can be created (*Customize your term set*), as shown in Figure 5-27. Logically, the second option mentioned must be chosen. The root concept named *Taxonomy* already exists. To create new terms, the user must click the already existing concept. Afterward, the *Create Term* menu appears. By clicking this button, a subordinated term can be created. This allows the whole taxonomy to be created as a term set of this SharePoint library. After adding this column to the library, the new column is added to the view.

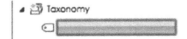

Figure 5-27. Adding a workflow to a SharePoint application

- **Exercise 5.1.3—Understand "Metadata Document Library":** Adding new documents to a document library can be performed in different ways. The easiest way is to just drag and drop an existing document (e.g., an Excel file) into the library. After dropping the document into the library, the *Name* of the file appears, including the data for the columns *Modified* and *Modified By*. However, the column created in the previous exercise is not automatically filled, as we did not specify a *Default value*. To fill the column for the uploaded document, the document must be chosen from the library, before the *Edit Properties* button has to be clicked. A new page appears to edit the properties of the document. Here, a *Title* can be specified, apart from the already automatically defined *Name* of the file. In addition, the value for the column *Taxonomy* can be specified (see Figure 5-28). After clicking the *Term Set* symbol, a pop up appears that includes the taxonomy specified for this column. Now, the concept (term) required can be selected and, through this, can be added to the column of this document. After all files (documents) are uploaded to the *Document Library*, the column *Document Taxonomy* can be used to formally filter for all documents satisfying a taxonomical search query. Here there are different options. The search can include exactly one concept (term), or the query can be extended to also filter for terms being parent terms of other terms.

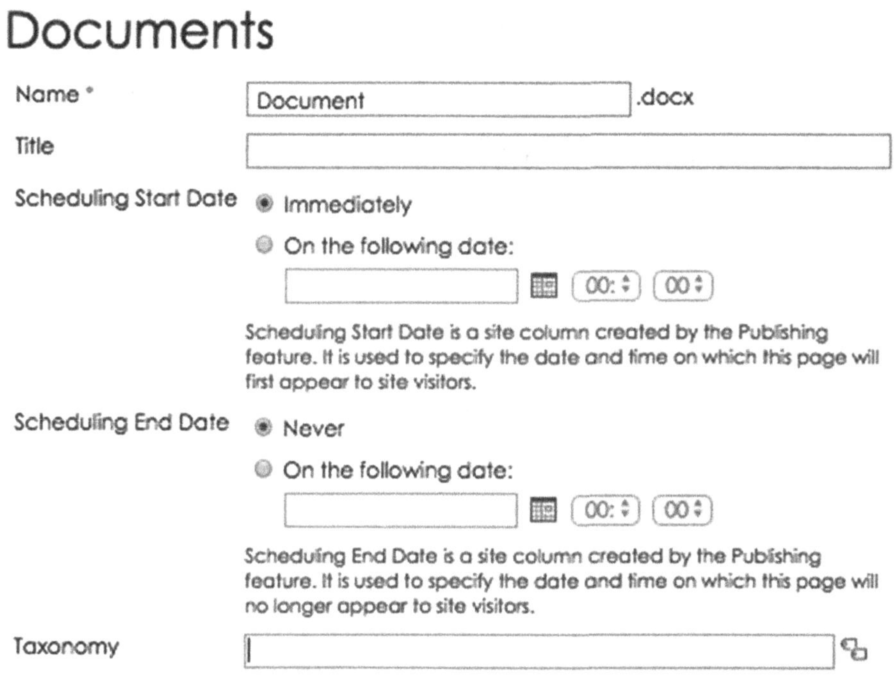

Documents

Name *		.docx

Name * ⬚ Document .docx

Title ⬚

Scheduling Start Date ◉ Immediately
⬚ ○ On the following date:
⬚ 📅 (00: ⬍) (00 ⬍)

Scheduling Start Date is a site column created by the Publishing feature. It is used to specify the date and time on which this page will first appear to site visitors.

Scheduling End Date ◉ Never
⬚ ○ On the following date:
⬚ 📅 (00: ⬍) (00 ⬍)

Scheduling End Date is a site column created by the Publishing feature. It is used to specify the date and time on which this page will no longer appear to site visitors.

Taxonomy ⬚

Figure 5-28. Specifying the term for formally classifying an item or document

Use Case 5.2: Using Enterprise Metadata Techniques

Enterprise Metadata is often also used in libraries and lists. This type of metadata is useful to further describe a document or item. The solutions for the exercises are as follows:

- **Exercise 5.2.1—Allow "Enterprise Metadata"**: For each list and library, enterprise keywords can be added to the application. To do this, *Library Settings* must be used, as well as the included settings in *Enterprise Metadata and Keywords Settings* (see Figure 5-29). After clicking this setting, a new page appears, including the section named *Add Enterprise Keywords*. By clicking the check box, an *Enterprise Keywords* column will be added to the library. However, this column is not automatically added to the *Current View*. This can be performed by using the *Modify View* button and choosing the column named *Enterprise Keywords* from the section named *Columns*. Adding *Enterprise Keywords* to existing documents can be performed by using the *Edit Properties* button. After clicking this button, a new page appears, from which the *Enterprise Keywords* can be specified (see Figure 5-30). The keywords can be used to filter for client-specific documents, for example.

Enterprise Metadata and Keywords Settings

Add Enterprise Keywords

An enterprise keywords column allows users to enter one or more text values that will be shared with other users and applications to allow for ease of search and filtering, as well as metadata consistency and reuse.

Adding an Enterprise Keywords column also provides synchronization between existing legacy keyword fields and the managed metadata infrastructure. (Document tags will be copied into the Enterprise Keywords on upload.)

Enterprise Keywords

☑ Add an Enterprise Keywords column to this list and enable Keyword synchronization

Figure 5-29. Adding enterprise keywords to a SharePoint application

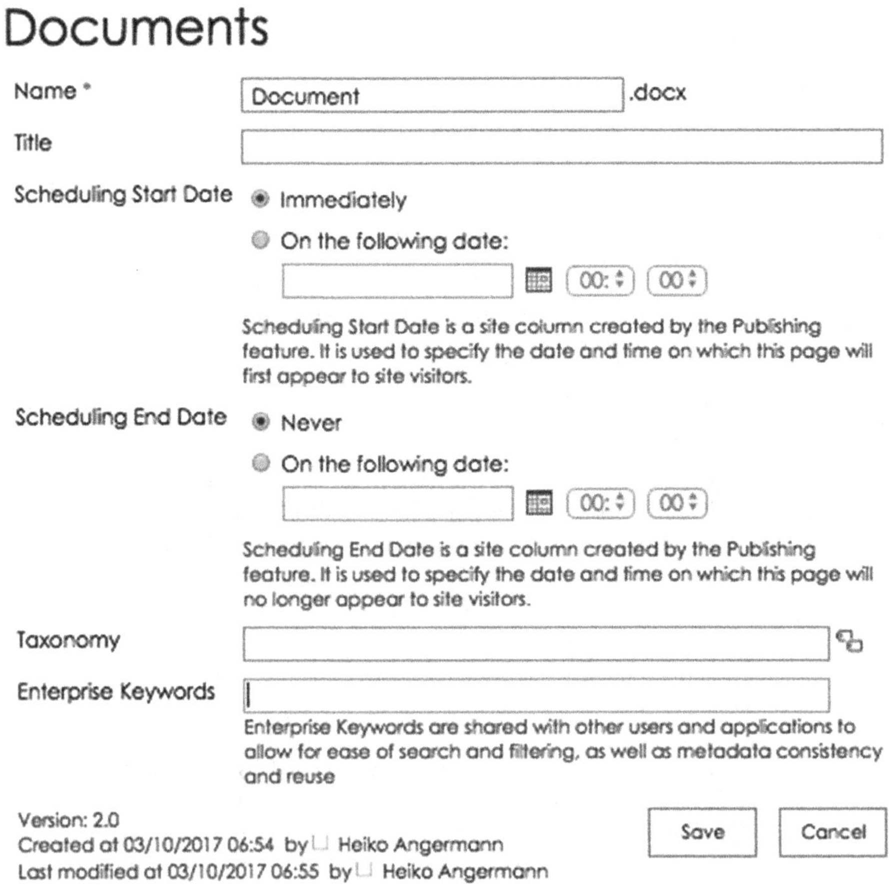

Documents

Name *	Document	.docx
Title		

Scheduling Start Date   ● Immediately

○ On the following date:

[　　　　　] 🗓 (00: ⇕) (00 ⇕)

Scheduling Start Date is a site column created by the Publishing feature. It is used to specify the date and time on which this page will first appear to site visitors.

Scheduling End Date   ● Never

○ On the following date:

[　　　　　] 🗓 (00: ⇕) (00 ⇕)

Scheduling End Date is a site column created by the Publishing feature. It is used to specify the date and time on which this page will no longer appear to site visitors.

Taxonomy   [　　　　　　　　　　　　　　　　] 🔗

Enterprise Keywords | [　　　　　　　　　　　　　　　　]

Enterprise Keywords are shared with other users and applications to allow for ease of search and filtering, as well as metadata consistency and reuse

Version: 2.0
Created at 03/10/2017 06:54 by⊔ Heiko Angermann
Last modified at 03/10/2017 06:55 by⊔ Heiko Angermann

[Save]   [Cancel]

Figure 5-30. Specifying the keywords for informally classifying an item or document

- **Exercise 5.2.2—Integrate "Three State Workflow"**: Adding a new column to the library can be performed with the *Create Column* button. Afterward, a new pop up appears, from which the *Name and Type* of the column to be created can be specified. Here, the type *Choice* should be chosen. The most important section for this type of column is *Additional Column Settings*, more precisely the included field named *Type each choice on a separate line*. Using this, the choices being allowed can be specified. By default, three choices already exist, which have only to be renamed as required. Below, the display choice *Drop-Down Menu* can be specified, and then the *Default value* should be *Draft*. After clicking *OK*, the new column is added to the current view.

- **Exercise 5.2.3—Start "Three State Workflow"**: By clicking the *Workflow Settings* button, a new page with the same name appears. Here, a button exists to *Add a Workflow*. After clicking this button, the user is forwarded to a new page, also having the same name as the button. In the first section, named *Workflow*, the desired workflow to be added to the library can be specified, which is for our tutorial of the type *Three State*. Using the section below named *Name*, the name for the workflow, which is *Document Status*, can be specified. That a new item added to the library is to start this workflow can be specified in *Start Options*. After clicking *OK*, a new page appears to *Customize the Three-state workflow* (see Figure 5-31).

Add or Change a Workflow ▸ Customize the …

Workflow states:

Select a 'Choice' field, and then select a value for the initial, middle, and final states. For an Issues list, the states for an item are specified by the Status field, where:
Initial State = Active
Middle State = Resolved
Final State = Closed
As the item moves through the various stages of the workflow, the item is updated automatically.

Select a 'Choice' field:

| Three_x0020_State | ⬍ |

Initial state

| State 1 (Draft) #1 | ⬍ |

Middle state

| State 2 (Finished) #2 | ⬍ |

Final state

| State 3 (Accepted) #3 | ⬍ |

Figure 5-31. Customizing the SharePoint three-state workflow

Solution 6: Improving Search Experience

In SharePoint, the Enterprise Search Center template provides an improved search experience. It can be used, with fine granularity, to modify the search mechanism according to an enterprise's needs. To do this, a new site or site-collection must be created. Afterward, replacement of the existing search center with the improved search center must be specified.

Use Case 6.1: Creating Enterprise Search Center

For creating a place to improve search experience, the accompanying site must be created in advance. This type of site additionally provides techniques to modify the search experience and, ultimately, to help find the desired information at the right time. To allow such techniques, the accompanying feature has to be activated. The solutions for the exercises are as follows:

- **Exercise 6.1.1—Add "Enterprise Search Center":** For activating the feature to allow modification of the search center, *Site Settings* must be used. After navigating to the *Site Collection Administration*, then the *Site Collection Features* section, the desired site appears. Here, the *SharePoint Server Publishing Infrastructure* feature can be activated. Afterward, the new subsite must be created. After clicking *new subsite*, a part of *Site Contents*, a new page appears. Here, the type of SharePoint site to be created can be chosen (see Figure 5-32). This type differs, depending on the template selected. In the first section, a *Title* and *Description* for the site to be created can be specified. Below, is the section named *Web Site Address*. Here, the *URL name* of the site to be created must be defined. Below is the *Template Selection* section. Here, a language for the subsite to be created can be defined. In addition, and most important, the template can be selected in this section. Four types of templates are listed: *Collaboration, Enterprise, Publishing*, and *Duet Enterprise*. The template for the search center to be created, which is named *Enterprise Search Center*, is listed under *Enterprise*. In the section below, *Permissions* can be specified. Here, users can decide to *Use same permissions as parent site*. The final section is *Navigation Inheritance*. Here, it can be specified if the subsite to be created has the same top link bar as provided in the parent site. After clicking *Create*, the new subsite of the type *Enterprise Search Center* is created.

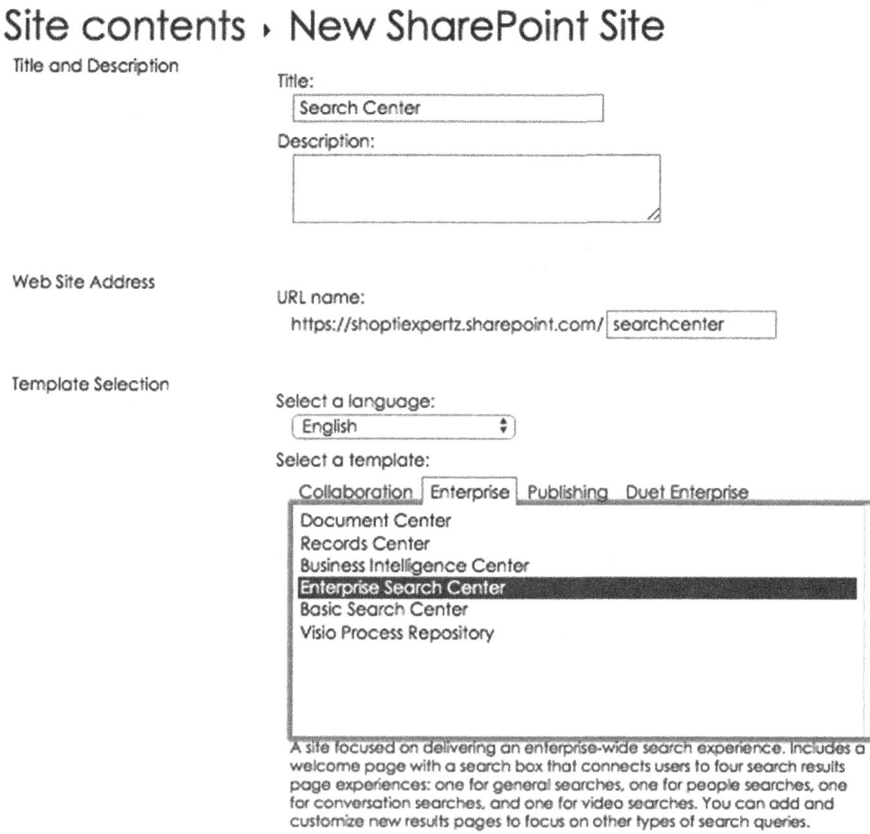

Site contents ᐟ New SharePoint Site

Title and Description

Title:

Search Center

Description:

Web Site Address

URL name:

https://shoptiexpertz.sharepoint.com/ searchcenter

Template Selection

Select a language:

English

Select a template:

Collaboration   Enterprise   Publishing   Duet Enterprise

Document Center
Records Center
Business Intelligence Center
Enterprise Search Center
Basic Search Center
Visio Process Repository

A site focused on delivering an enterprise-wide search experience. Includes a
welcome page with a search box that connects users to four search results
page experiences: one for general searches, one for people searches, one
for conversation searches, and one for video searches. You can add and
customize new results pages to focus on other types of search queries.

Figure 5-32. Adding an enterprise search center to a SharePoint site collection

- **Exercise 6.1.2—Modify "Search URL"**: After
  navigating to the *Search Settings* of the top-level site, a
  new page appears. This page includes two sections. The
  first section, named *Enter a Search Center URL*, defines
  the search center by its URL. Here, the URL of the
  site created above must be typed. The second section
  asks for the results page the queries should be sent to.
  Here, we decide to *Use the same results page settings as my
  parent*. This means that the search center is replacing the
  initial search center existing on the parent site and that a
  second results page is not created.

- **Exercise 6.1.3—Analyze "Result Page"**: Typing a query on the top-level site forwards the user to the result page defined in the preceding exercise. The page consists of five main areas, shown in Figure 5-33. At the top, the search slot is displayed, including the queried string. Below, specification can be initiated, using one of four refiners. By clicking one of the refiners, the query is refined to the underlying content type, except if *Everything* is defined, which is the default refiner. Below the refiners, the search results are shown. In addition to the name of the search result, its link is shown. When hovering over a search result, an extraction of the result is shown. On the bottom of the page, below the search results, search statistics are shown. This highlights how many search results have been found. In addition, more settings can be performed, including the following: *Alert Me*, *Preferences*, and *Advanced Search*. The fifth section provides faceted search techniques. Three facets are provided: *Result type*, *Author*, and *Modified date*. Those facets can be used to additionally refine the search results.

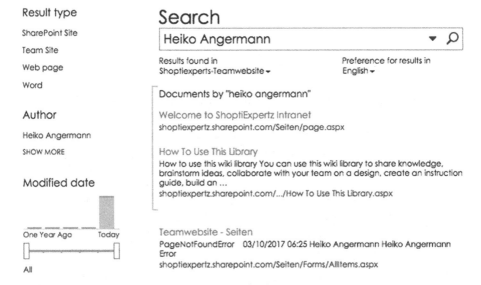

Figure 5-33. A typical result page as part of a SharePoint search center

Use Case 6.2: Customizing Search Center

For creating a place to improve search experience, the accompanying site has to be created in advance. This type of site additionally provides techniques to modify the search experience and, ultimately, to help find the desired information at the right time. To allow such techniques, the accompanying feature has to be activated. The solutions for the exercises are as follows:

- **Exercise 6.2.1—Customize "Result Page"**: The result page is analogous to other SharePoint pages. It is mainly a collection of web parts providing different services, as shown in Figure 5-34. With these, editing the results page is equal to editing another SharePoint page. To do this, *Edit Page* has to be clicked. Afterward, the page will be checked out, which allows users to edit the existing web parts and to add new web parts. The web parts already included on the page are divided into zones. Two zones exist: *Navigation Zone* and *Main Zone*. In the first mentioned zone, the web part *Refinement* is included, in which the facets can be edited or new refiners added. In *Main Zone*, three web parts are included: *Search Box*, *Search Navigation*, and *Search Results*. The web part *Search Box* shows the search slot. The web part *Search Navigation* allows for showing and editing the refiners. The last web part, *Search Results*, is responsible for displaying the search results. The settings for this web part can be edited by clicking *Edit Web Part*. The *Settings* are part of the *Properties for Search Results* section. By clicking *Settings*, different check boxes are shown that can modify the settings for the search results. The check boxes are classified in two sections: *Results settings* and *Results control settings*. To specify that duplicate links should be displayed, the accompanying check box, which is *Show View Duplicate link* in the section *Results settings*, must be clicked. To specify that the drop down can be sorted, another check box has to be clicked, which is named *Show sort dropdown*, of the *Results control settings* section. All mentioned *Settings* are part of the *Properties for Search Results*. In addition to the *Settings*, the *Search Criteria* can be edited, as well as the *Display Templates*. Other modifications that can be performed when editing this web part are *Appearance*, *Layout*, and *Advanced*.

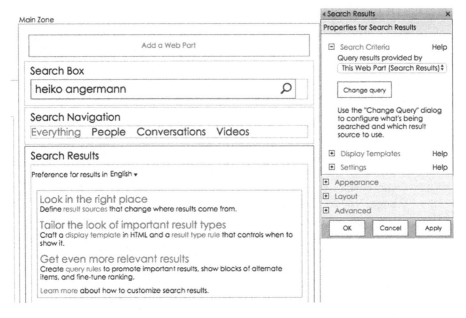

Figure 5-34. Editing a SharePoint result page using web parts

- **Exercise 6.2.2—Customize "Faceted Search"**: The *Refinement* web part is shown in the *Navigation Zone*. By clicking *Edit Web Part*, the refiners (facets) can be specified (see Figure 5-35). Under *Properties for Search Refinement*, the refiners can be chosen. After clicking the previously mentioned button, a pop up appears. Here, an overview of all available refiners is listed vs. an overview of all selected refiners. By default, six refiners are chosen: *File Type, Content Class, Content Type Id, Web Template, Display Author,* and *Last Modified Time*. The refiners named *Languages, Size,* and *Tags* are not yet selected. To do this, they have to be searched under *Available refiners,* and by clicking on the refiner, they will be added to the *Selected refiners*. Resorting the refiners can be performed by using *Move up* and *Move down* buttons. By clicking one of the refiners listed in *Selected refiners,* these can be configured in detail. By clicking the *Languages* refiner, the following configurations can be performed: *Display name, Display template, Sort by, Sort direction,* and *Maximum number of refiner values*. Logically, the last configuration mentioned is required to limit the maximum number of refiner values. Clicking the refiner named *Size* allows for the following configurations to be performed: *Display name,*

Display template, and *Intervals*. By using *Display name*, the new name can be typed in a text box, which is *File size*. Clicking the refiner named *Tags* allows for the following configurations to be performed: *Display name*, *Display template*, *Sort by*, *Sort direction*, and *Maximum number of refiner values*. By using *Display template*, the required template can be defined.

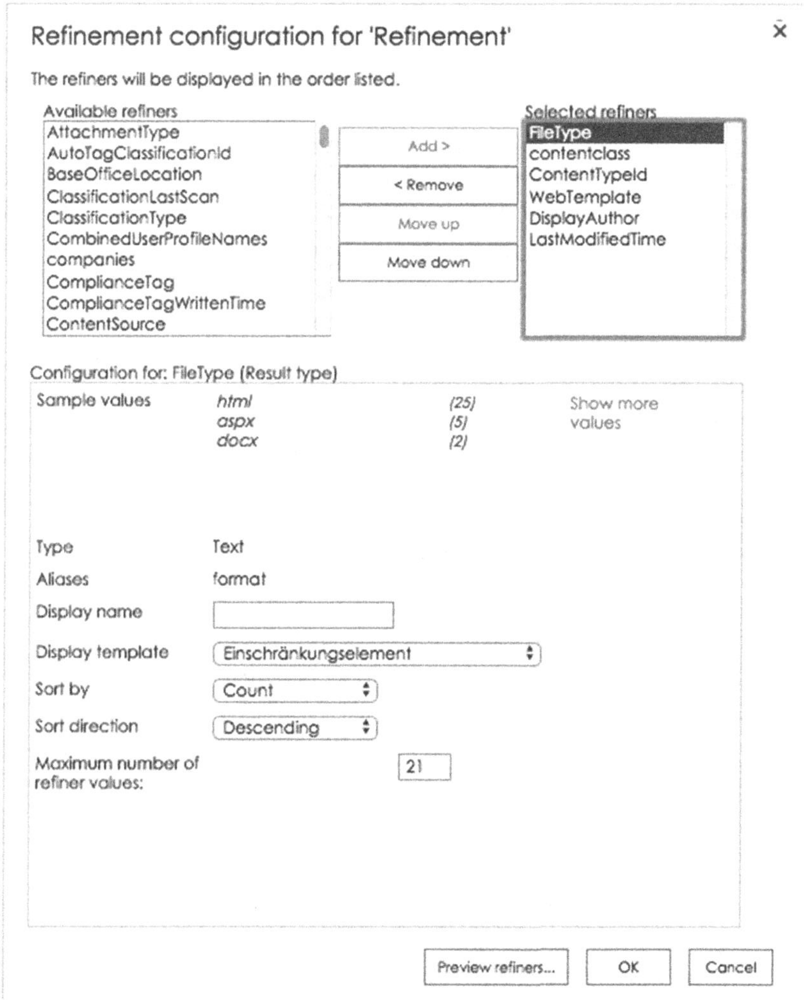

Figure 5-35. Editing the SharePoint refinement web part as part of the SharePoint result page

Solution 7: Managing Projects

In SharePoint, the Project Site template provides a project workspace. This can be used to administrate small and medium-sized projects. To apply this, a new site or site collection must be created. It is not recommended to have a project workspace as a site collection but, rather, as a site performing as a subsite of a site collection.

Use Case 7.1: Creating Tasks in Projects

For creating tasks in projects, the accompanying site must be created in advance. This type of site additionally provides a project dashboard summarizing important information about the project and its status. Finally, a project consisting of different tasks requires that the tasks be created in a separated application (app). The solutions for the exercises are as follows:

- **Exercise 7.1.1—Add "Project Workspace"**: After clicking *New subsite* a new page appears. On it, the type of SharePoint site to be created can be chosen. Types differ, depending on the template selected. In the first section, a *Title* and *Description* for the site to be created can be specified. Below is the section named *Web Site Address*. Here, the *URL name* of the site to be created must be defined. Below is *Template Selection*. Here, a language for the subsite to be created can be defined. In addition, and most important, the template can be selected in this section. Four types of templates are listed: *Collaboration*, *Enterprise*, *Publishing*, and *Duet Enterprise*. The template for the project workspace to be created, which is named *Project Workspace*, is listed under *Collaboration*. In the section below, *Permissions* can be specified. Here, users decide to *Use same permissions as parent site*. The final section is *Navigation Inheritance*. From here, whether the subsite to be created is to have the same top link bar as provided in the parent site can be specified. After clicking *Create*, the new subsite of the type *Project Site* is created.

- **Exercise 7.1.2—Manage "Project Dashboard"**: The project workspace can be added as a link to the top-level site, by navigating to the top-level site and clicking *Edit Links*, a part of the local navigation. After clicking the button, existing links can be removed or edited, by clicking the name of the link. In addition, links can be added. For links to be added, the URL of the page (subsite) must be defined, and a name provided. When navigating to the subsite created, a start page is displayed. Below the title of the subsite, which is *Project Workspace*, a *Project Summary* is shown. The summary is shown as a time line. Below, a section named *Get started with your site* is displayed. To modify the site, the user can click the buttons shown (see Figure 5-36). Below, another section shows documents. This section is based on a document library including the latest documents to be added to this subsite. At the bottom of the summary page, is a *Newsfeed*. This aims to display the most recent conversations occurring on the subsite.

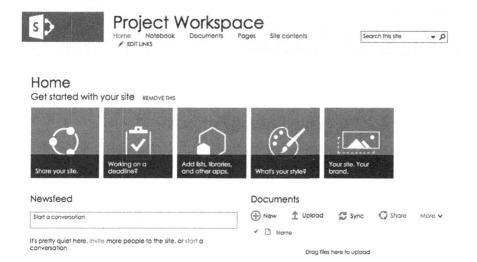

Figure 5-36. The starting page of a project workspace in SharePoint

- **Exercise 7.1.3—Manage "Main Project Tasks"**: The *Tasks* list is based on a SharePoint list application (see Figure 5-37). The application consists of two parts. The first part shows a time line. In the second part, tasks, i.e., list items, can be created. To create tasks, the New Item button, which forwards the user to a new page, must be clicked. Here, the task to be created can be managed by different columns: *Task Name*, *Start Date*, *Due Date*, and *Assigned To*. In the first column, names of the task, *Task A* and *Task B*, respectively, can be defined. The following two columns are not mandatory. The fourth column assigns the task to a specific person, e.g., the product owner of the project. By clicking *Show More*, the tasks to be created can be specified in more detail: *% Complete*,

Description, Predecessors, Priority, and Task Status. Using the Predecessors column, dependencies between tasks can be specified. In our example, for Task B, the Predecessors is Task A.

Tasks

Figure 5-37. Adding tasks as items of the task list in SharePoint

Use Case 7.2: Managing Tasks in Projects

For effectively managing tasks in projects, it is often required to link tasks to other tasks, as a task often consists of other tasks. In addition, the tasks are often performed by different teams. The solutions for the exercises are as follows:

- **Exercise 7.2.1—Manage "Sub Tasks":** By clicking a task (item) in the *Tasks* list, a pop up appears. Here, the *Create Sub task* button is included. After clicking this button, a new item is automatically added to the list, which is listed below the item for which the subtask is created (see Figure 5-38). For each subtask, a name must be defined. The subtasks are not automatically assigned to a specific person. In fact, they are not assigned to anyone. To additionally assign subtasks to persons, the subtask has to be opened, and the accompanying column has to be filled.

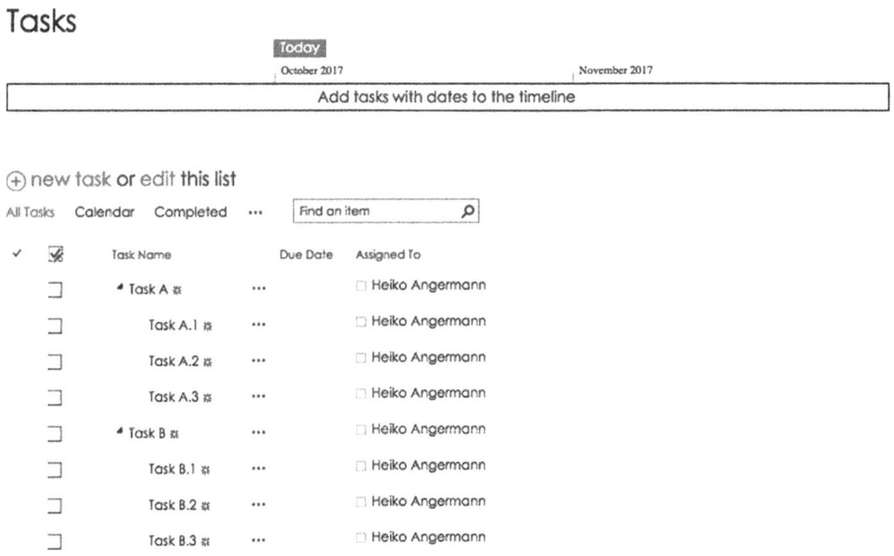

Tasks

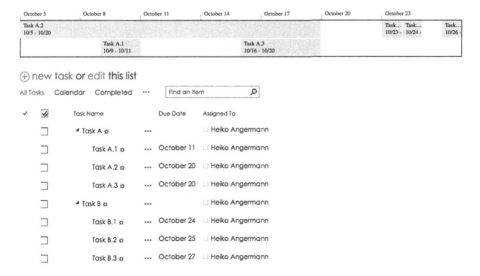

Figure 5-38. Adding subtasks to tasks

- **Exercise 7.2.2—Manage "Project Timeline"**:A *Start Date* and a *Due Date*, respectively, can be added to each task and subtask when editing the list item when opening the subtask. By clicking the task, these can be added to the time line (see Figure 5-39).

Tasks

Figure 5-39. Adding subtasks and/or tasks to the project time line

Conclusion

This chapter presented different hands-on solutions to experience the capabilities of Microsoft's latest SharePoint release, Microsoft SharePoint Server 2016, practically. All presented solutions have been based on the hands-on tutorials presented in chapter 3. As such, a user can check her/his own performance or can use the individual sections to look up partial steps. For each solution, various use cases have been discussed. The solutions for the tutorials have been presented in a very comprehensive manner, supported by adding screenshots for the most important tasks to be performed. After a user has performed the tutorials in chapter 3, and has studied the solutions presented in the chapter at hand, she/he will be able to perform the most common SharePoint operations.

Conclusions

This book has provided a hands-on introduction to the enterprise content management system SharePoint Server 2016. In this chapter, the conclusions that have been reached are reviewed.

The book began, in the first chapter, with an informative introduction to the general principles of content management. This included an explanation of the logical components of content management systems (CMS), the basic requirements for supporting finding information, as well as an introduction to the different types of CMS on the market. In addition, the chapter outlined the different types of licenses and provision models used to implement and operate a CMS and gave an overview of the available evaluation and research methodologies most widely used by enterprises.

In the second chapter, the technologies provided by SharePoint and its principal areas were reviewed. This included the basic elements of SharePoint, the core technologies always required to implement and customize the system, an explanation of the included technology to improve social networking, as well as an overview of the different types of administration levels. In addition, the templates provided out of the box were explored in detail, for each type of site and site collection template (collaboration templates, enterprise templates, and publishing templates). The most widely used templates also were comprehensively reviewed.

To practically experience the capabilities of SharePoint, hands-on tutorials based on real-world scenarios were presented in the third chapter. This chapter began with an introduction to the methodology being used to present the tutorials and the underlying idea, as well as the preparations required to perform the tutorials. Afterward, the tutorials were finally presented.

© Heiko Angermann 2017
H. Angermann, *Manager's Guide to SharePoint Server 2016*,
https://doi.org/10.1007/978-1-4842-3045-9_6

In all, seven tutorials, including various use cases, were presented, covering the principal areas of SharePoint: managing users, improving social networking, customizing the look and feel, integrating applications, using metadata technologies, improving search experience, and managing tasks.

Based on the SharePoint technology presented in the second chapter, best practice scenarios were presented in the fourth chapter. Such best practices give advice concerning what is important before implementing SharePoint and after the system has been set up. The chapter began with best practices regarding how to set up and maintain a governance model, including how to set up a governance committee and the elements of a governance plan. Afterward, best practices regarding the use of the site and site collection templates were presented, including the use and differences related to collaboration, enterprise, and publishing templates. Finally, best practices regarding the use of additional tools were given. Here, tools provided by Microsoft to help customize the system, as well as tools provided by third party providers to improve workflows, to simplify the usage of external data sources, as well as for better managing metadata, were reviewed.

Using the fifth chapter, solutions to the tutorials presented in the third chapter were given. Again, the chapter began with an introduction to the methodology being used to present the solutions. Afterward, the solutions for the different areas of SharePoint were provided in detail. Again, the solutions were divided into single use cases. In all, solutions for 15 use cases were presented. The most important use cases presented were the following: managing site owners' and users' permissions, maintaining My Site profiles and using My Site features, using and customizing SharePoint, using applications and workflows, using metadata techniques, creating and customizing search centers, and creating and managing tasks in projects.

Index

T, U, V

W, X, Y, Z

Get the eBook for only $5!

Why limit yourself?

With most of our titles available in both PDF and ePUB format, you can access your content wherever and however you wish—on your PC, phone, tablet, or reader.

Since you've purchased this print book, we are happy to offer you the eBook for just $5.

To learn more, go to http://www.apress.com/companion or contact support@apress.com.

Apress®

Printed in the United States
By Bookmasters